RICHARD LUNDY

NEW ORLEANS TRAVEL GUIDE 2024-2025

Exploring the Must-See Attractions, Accommodations and Itineraries

Copyright © 2024 by Richard Lundy

All rights reserved. No part of this publication may be reproduced, stored or transmitted in any form or by any means, electronic, mechanical, photocopying, recording, scanning, or otherwise without written permission from the publisher. It is illegal to copy this book, post it to a website, or distribute it by any other means without permission.

Richard Lundy asserts the moral right to be identified as the author of this work.

First edition

This book was professionally typeset on Reedsy. Find out more at reedsy.com

Contents

Introduction	1
About This Guide	1
History of New Orleans	3
Chapter 1: Planning Your Trip	5
Best Time to Visit	5
Visa and Entry Requirements	7
Packing Essentials	9
Transportation Options	12
Chapter 2: Must-See Attractions	15
The French Quarter	15
Jackson Square	16
The National WWII Museum	18
Frenchmen Street	20
The Garden District	21
A Swamp Tour	23
St. Louis Cathedral	26
City Park	27
Audubon Zoo and Aquarium of the Americas	29
Café du Monde	31
Chapter 3: Culinary Delights and Cultural Experiences	33
Iconic New Orleans Dishes	33
Best Restaurants and Cafes	34
Festivals and Events	38
Chapter 4: Accommodations in New Orleans	40
Rental Apartments	40
Hotels and Hostels	43

Chapter 5: Outdoor Activities and Recreation	47
Parks and Gardens	47
Swamp Tours	49
Riverboat Cruises	51
Walking and Bike Tours	53
Chapter 6: Nightlife in New Orleans	56
Bars, Clubs and Live Music Venues	56
Theatres and Performing Arts	59
Chapter 7: Shopping in New Orleans	62
Local Markets	62
Souvenir Shops	64
Art and Antique Stores	66
Chapter 8: Day Trips and Excursions	69
Plantations	69
Nearby Cities and Towns	71
Coastal Adventures	73
Chapter 9: Planning Your Itinerary	77
A 7-Day General Itinerary	77
A 3-Day Romantic Itinerary for Couples	81
A 5-Day Culinary Itinerary	84
Chapter 10: Practical Information and Tips	88
Language and Communication	88
Currency and Money Matters	90
Health and Safety Tips	92
Conclusion	95

Introduction

About This Guide

Welcome to the NEW ORLEANS TRAVEL GUIDE 2024-2025: Discovering the Top Attractions, Accommodations, and Itineraries! This all-inclusive guide is designed to help you plan an unforgettable visit to the Big Easy, catering to all interests and budgets. Whether you love history, food, music, or vibrant cultural experiences, New Orleans has something for everyone.

This guide provides all the essential information for a smooth trip from 2024 to 2025, helping you make the most of the city's famous festivals and events. We'll explore New Orleans' rich history in the next section, but first, here's what this guide offers:

1. Must-See Attractions: From the iconic French Quarter and Jackson Square to the enchanting swamp tours, we'll cover major landmarks and hidden gems like the Garden District and City Park.

2. Culinary Delights and Cultural Experiences: Dive into the city's lively culinary scene with dishes like Po'Boys and Gumbo, and must-try drinks like the Sazerac. We'll also highlight local traditions, upcoming festivals, and cultural treasures.

3. Accommodations: Discover the best places to stay, whether you're looking for a cosy Bed and Breakfast, a luxurious hotel, or a budget-friendly hostel.

4. Outdoor Activities and Recreation: New Orleans offers more than just history and food! We'll recommend parks, riverboat cruises, and scenic walking and biking tours.

5. Nightlife and Entertainment: Experience the legendary live music on Frenchmen Street, explore hidden speakeasies, or enjoy a show at one of the city's theatres.

6. Shopping: From bustling markets with unique souvenirs to art galleries featuring local artists, we'll guide you through the city's diverse shopping options.

7. Day Trips and Excursions: Enhance your New Orleans visit with day trips to nearby plantations, charming towns, or coastal getaways.

8. Planning Your Itinerary: Overwhelmed by options? We've got pre-designed itineraries for different interests, including a 7-day general itinerary, a romantic couples' escape, or a 5-day culinary tour. Customise these to suit your interests and schedule.

9. Practical Information and Tips: Find valuable advice on navigating the city, understanding local customs, key phrases, and ensuring a safe and enjoyable trip.

This guide is your gateway to the wonders of New Orleans. Let's embark on this adventure together and see why this city continues to captivate travellers from around the globe.

INTRODUCTION

* * *

History of New Orleans

New Orleans boasts a history as rich and vibrant as its renowned jazz music. To grasp the city's unique character, one must delve into its fascinating past, marked by French ambition, Spanish influence, resilience in adversity, and the enduring spirit of its people.

French Beginnings (1718 - 1763)

In 1718, French explorer Jean-Baptiste Le Moyne de Bienville founded New Orleans, strategically located on a crescent-shaped bend of the Mississippi River. Named after the Duke of Orléans, the city was envisioned as a pivotal port to control trade routes and expand French colonial power in North America. French architects meticulously designed the city, establishing the iconic grid layout of the French Quarter with its wrought-iron balconies and colourful facades. The early years were challenging, with disease outbreaks, floods, and conflicts with Native American tribes threatening the fledgling settlement. Despite these hardships, French culture thrived, focusing on art, music, and culinary excellence, which continue to define New Orleans today. The arrival of enslaved Africans in 1719 not only provided forced labour for the colony's development but also laid the groundwork for a unique cultural blend that would become a hallmark of the city.

Spanish Rule (1763 - 1803)

After France's defeat in the Seven Years' War, New Orleans and Louisiana were ceded to Spain in 1763. Spanish rule brought a more relaxed social atmosphere and an increased influence of Catholicism. The city's architecture also evolved, with buildings like the St. Louis Cathedral showcasing Spanish colonial styles. During this period, a distinct class system emerged, including the "gens de couleur libres" (free people of colour), born from relationships between Europeans and enslaved Africans. This group significantly shaped the city's cultural identity, especially its vibrant music scene.

The Louisiana Purchase and Beyond (1803 - Present)

In 1803, the United States acquired New Orleans through the Louisiana Purchase from Napoleon Bonaparte, marking a turning point for the city as it became part of the growing American nation. The 19th century saw immense growth for New Orleans, driven by its role as a major port city for cotton exports. However, this prosperity was marred by the continued entrenchment of slavery, casting a dark shadow on the city's progress.

Challenges and Triumphs

Throughout its history, New Orleans has faced numerous challenges. The devastating yellow fever epidemics of the 18th and 19th centuries and countless floods, most notably Hurricane Katrina in 2005, took a heavy toll. Yet, New Orleans has consistently shown remarkable resilience, rebuilding stronger after each setback.

Today, New Orleans stands as a testament to its multicultural heritage, shaped by French, Spanish, African, and American influences. The vibrant music scene, from soulful jazz to the lively rhythms of Mardi Gras, reflects this rich tapestry. The city's cuisine, blending European and African traditions, is a true melting pot of flavours.

Understanding New Orleans' history allows visitors to appreciate the depth and complexity woven into the fabric of this remarkable city. From its colonial beginnings to its enduring spirit, New Orleans continues to captivate visitors with its rich cultural heritage, joie de vivre (joy of living), and unwavering resilience.

Chapter 1: Planning Your Trip

Best Time to Visit

New Orleans welcomes visitors year-round, but the best time for your trip depends on your priorities. Here's a breakdown of each season's pros and cons to help you decide.

Spring (March – May)

- Pros: Spring offers pleasant weather, with average temperatures in the 70s (Fahrenheit), perfect for outdoor exploration. Crowds are smaller, and hotel rates are generally more affordable. Plus, the renowned New Orleans Jazz & Heritage Festival in April/May celebrates the city's musical heritage.

- Cons: Spring can bring occasional rain showers, so pack an umbrella. Late spring sees rising temperatures and higher humidity. Some major events like Mardi Gras are already over.

Summer (June – August)

- Pros: Summer features the hottest weather, with average highs in the 80s (Fahrenheit) and plenty of sunshine, ideal for outdoor activities like riverboat cruises and swamp tours.

- Cons: The heat and humidity can be overwhelming, especially for those not used to a subtropical climate. It's peak tourist season, leading to larger crowds and higher hotel rates. Afternoon thunderstorms are also common.

Fall (September - November)

- Pros: Fall offers a break from the summer heat, with cooling temperatures and decreasing humidity. It's a great time for walking tours and outdoor festivals, like the French Quarter Fest in October. Crowds thin out, and accommodation deals are more available.

- Cons: Fall weather can be unpredictable, with occasional rain showers and the potential for hurricanes. Some events might be winding down for the season.

Winter (December - February)

- Pros: Winter is the coolest and driest season, with comfortable temperatures in the 50s (Fahrenheit) and minimal rain. Sightseeing is pleasant without summer crowds, and hotel rates are typically the lowest. The holiday season offers unique celebrations like Christmas Eve bonfires on the levee.

- Cons: Some festivals and attractions may have limited hours or be closed during winter. The festive atmosphere might not be as vibrant outside the holiday season.

Additional factors to consider

1. Mardi Gras: This famous celebration usually falls in February or early March. If Mardi Gras is a priority, plan your trip accordingly but expect larger crowds and higher prices.

2. Festivals and Events: New Orleans hosts vibrant festivals year-round. Check the festival calendar to align your visit with events that interest you.

Ultimately, the best time to visit New Orleans depends on your personal preferences. Consider your preferred weather, budget, and any specific events you'd like to experience when planning your trip.

Visa and Entry Requirements

Whether you're eager to explore the French Quarter's lively streets or savour the city's famous beignets at Café Du Monde, understanding visa and entry requirements is essential for a smooth arrival in New Orleans. This section will guide you through the process, ensuring a hassle-free start to your adventure.

Do You Need a Visa?

The United States operates a Visa Waiver Program (VWP) that allows citizens of certain countries to enter for tourism or business purposes for up to 90 days without a visa. However, there's an important step involved:

1. Electronic System for Travel Authorization (ESTA): Citizens from VWP

countries must apply for ESTA authorization online at least 72 hours before departure. ESTA applications are straightforward, requiring basic information like passport details and travel plans. A small fee applies. While approval typically occurs within a few days, it's wise to apply well in advance.

If You Don't Qualify for VWP

If your country isn't part of the VWP, you'll need to obtain a visa from a U.S. embassy or consulate in your home country. The visa application process can be more complex, often requiring an interview and additional documentation. Contact your nearest U.S. embassy or consulate well in advance for specific instructions and processing times.

General Entry Requirements

Here's a checklist of essential documents for all travellers entering the U.S.:

1. Valid Passport: Your passport must be valid for at least six months beyond your intended departure date from the United States. Some countries may have different requirements, so check with the U.S. Department of State or your home country's embassy/consulate.

2. Proof of Onward or Return Ticket: This demonstrates your intention to leave the U.S. after your visit.

3. ESTA Approval (if applicable): Have your ESTA approval ready for presentation upon arrival if travelling under the VWP.

4. Visa (if required): Present your valid visa if you don't qualify for VWP entry.

Additional Considerations

1. Customs Declaration Form: You may need to complete a Customs Declaration Form on the plane or upon arrival, detailing items you're bringing into the U.S.

2. Vaccinations: While not mandatory for most visitors, some vaccinations may be recommended depending on your origin country. Consult with your healthcare professional or the Centers for Disease Control and Prevention (CDC) for the latest recommendations.

Staying Informed

For the most current and official information on visa and entry requirements, check the U.S. Department of State's Bureau of Consular Affairs website and the U.S. Customs and Border Protection (CBP) website

* * *

Packing Essentials

New Orleans is a city that thrives on a vibrant mix of cultures, reflected in its lively music scene, delectable cuisine, and exciting festivals. To ensure you pack the perfect essentials for your trip, consider the following factors.

Climate

New Orleans has a subtropical climate, with hot and humid summers and mild winters. For warmer months, pack breathable fabrics like cotton and linen. Evenings can be cooler, so a light jacket or sweater is recommended. During spring or fall, pack layers to accommodate temperature fluctuations.

Activities

Plan your outfits based on activities such as exploring the French Quarter, taking a swamp tour, or dancing on Frenchmen Street.

Walking

New Orleans is a pedestrian-friendly city, so comfortable walking shoes are a must. Choose shoes with good support for extended periods of walking.

Dress Code

New Orleans has a relaxed and casual vibe. Leave formal wear at home and pack comfortable clothing like t-shirts, shorts, skirts, or lightweight pants. For evenings, a slightly dressier outfit like jeans and a nice top is appropriate for most restaurants and bars.

Packing Checklist

Clothing

1. Casual t-shirts, tank tops, or blouses
2. Comfortable walking shoes
3. Sandals or flip-flops (optional)
4. Comfortable pants, skirts, or shorts (2-3 pairs)
5. Light jacket or sweater for evenings
6. Dressier outfit (optional)
7. Swimsuit (for pools, swamp tours, or the beach)
8. Pajamas and undergarments
9. Hat for sun protection

Accessories

1. Sunglasses
2. Sunscreen (SPF 30 or higher)
3. Insect repellent (especially in mosquito season)
4. Umbrella or rain jacket (summer showers)
5. Scarf (for warmth or as a cover-up in churches)
6. Small backpack for day trips

Toiletries

1. Travel-sized toiletries (shampoo, conditioner, soap, etc.)
2. Toothbrush, toothpaste, and personal hygiene items
3. Medications (if applicable)

Electronics

1. Phone charger
2. Portable power bank (optional)
3. Camera (optional)
4. Adapter plug (if travelling from outside the US)

Additional Tips

1. Pack light, breathable fabrics that dry quickly.
2. Roll clothes to save space in your luggage.
3. Bring a reusable water bottle to stay hydrated.
4. Pack an extra pair of shoes in case your primary pair gets wet.
5. Leave valuables at home and carry a small amount of cash.
6. Check the weather forecast before your trip to adjust your packing list accordingly.

* * *

Transportation Options

New Orleans boasts walkable neighbourhoods and essential attractions spread across the city. Choosing the right transportation depends on your budget, convenience, and distance.

Exploring on Foot

The best way to experience the heart of New Orleans, especially the French Quarter and the Garden District, is on foot. Walking allows you to enjoy the city's architectural beauty, vibrant street performers, and hidden gems. It's also budget-friendly and helps burn off calories from indulging in New Orleans' cuisine.

Biking

Renting a bicycle is a great way to explore the city actively. Several companies offer rentals, allowing you to see New Orleans at your own pace. Designated bike lanes and flat terrain make cycling feasible, particularly for places like City Park or the Mississippi Riverfront. Remember to stay mindful of traffic and wear a helmet.

Streetcars

The historic streetcar system is an iconic symbol of New Orleans and a charming way to travel. Streetcars have several lines that reach major attractions like St. Charles Avenue and Canal Street. Purchase a Jazzy Pass for unlimited rides during your stay.

Buses

The Regional Transit Authority (RTA) operates a comprehensive bus network that covers a broader area than streetcars. While not glamorous, buses are budget-friendly for reaching remote locations. Download the RTA app for real-time tracking and route planning. Buses can experience delays, so allow extra time.

Ride-Sharing Services

Uber and Lyft are convenient, especially at night or with luggage. They are more expensive than public transportation but ideal for quick trips or areas not well-served by buses or streetcars.

Taxis

Taxis are readily available in tourist areas and can be hailed on the street. Fares are typically higher than ride-sharing services. Agree on the fare beforehand or ensure the meter is running to avoid surprises.

Ferry

The Algiers Ferry offers a scenic journey across the Mississippi River, operating 24/7 with stunning views of the city skyline. It's a great way to explore Algiers Point, a historic neighbourhood with unique cultural charm.

Rental Cars

While not essential for the city centre, a rental car is beneficial for day trips or exploring plantations outside New Orleans. Consider parking costs and traffic congestion before deciding on a rental car.

Tips for Choosing Your Transportation

1. Location: If staying in the French Quarter or Warehouse District, most attractions are walkable. For farther locations, consider a mix of walking, streetcars, or buses.

2. Budget: Walking and public transportation are the most budget-friendly. Ride-sharing and taxis are more convenient but costlier. Factor in parking costs for rental cars.

3. Time: Walking and biking are slower. Streetcars and buses balance convenience and speed. Ride-sharing and taxis are quickest, especially during rush hour.

4. Group Size: Buses and streetcars suit solo travellers or small groups. For larger groups, taxis or ride-sharing might be more efficient.

Chapter 2: Must-See Attractions

The French Quarter

The French Quarter, affectionately known as the Vieux Carré (French for "Old Square"), is the heart of New Orleans. Enter this lively historic district, and you'll find yourself in a world of pastel-hued buildings with wrought-iron balconies, bustling narrow streets, and the captivating sounds of jazz drifting from famous venues.

Established in 1718, the French Quarter is New Orleans' oldest neighbourhood. The French and Spanish architectural influences are unmistakable, with charming townhouses boasting flower-filled courtyards and balconies. Jackson Square, a central point of interest, is surrounded by the grand St. Louis Cathedral, the historic Cabildo museum that delves into Louisiana's rich history, and the Presbytère with its local art and exhibits.

The French Quarter offers a delightful sensory experience. Street performers, from jazz musicians to colourful fortune tellers, entertain the crowds. The scent of freshly brewed coffee from iconic spots like Cafe du Monde mixes with the mouth-watering aromas of Creole and Cajun dishes from hidden restaurants. As evening falls, the area becomes a lively music hub, with live jazz pouring from legendary spots like Preservation Hall and Fritzel's Jazz Club.

While Bourbon Street is the most renowned (and occasionally notorious) part of the French Quarter, with its plethora of bars and neon lights, there are other treasures to explore. Royal Street is filled with art galleries and antique shops, while Frenchmen Street offers a more authentic live music experience. Discover charming courtyards like the one at the Pontalba Apartments, the oldest continuously occupied apartment building in the U.S.

A visit to the French Quarter isn't complete without seeing some of its iconic sights. Walk through Jackson Square, capture a photo with the stunning St. Louis Cathedral as your backdrop, and delve into the city's history at the Cabildo or the Presbytère. Enjoy a mule-drawn carriage ride for a delightful and informative tour of the district. Explore the intriguing world of voodoo at the New Orleans Historic Voodoo Museum.

Foodie Paradise

The French Quarter is a dream for food lovers. Enjoy classic beignets sprinkled with powdered sugar at Cafe du Monde, relish a hot bowl of gumbo or a decadent po'boy sandwich, or indulge in a multi-course Creole meal at a famous restaurant. Be sure to try local drinks like Hurricanes and Sazeracs, iconic cocktails that are synonymous with New Orleans.

* * *

Jackson Square

Jackson Square, situated at the heart of the French Quarter, is a lively landmark that captures the essence and history of New Orleans. Once known as Place d'Armes (French) or Plaza de Armas (Spanish), this 2.5-acre park has long been a hub of activity, serving as a gathering spot, marketplace, and focal point of city life for centuries. Today, it remains a must-visit destination for anyone wanting to experience the magic of New Orleans.

Established in 1721, Jackson Square has been integral to the city's evolution. It was the site of public executions, military parades, and bustling markets. After the War of 1812, it was renamed to honour Andrew Jackson, the hero of the Battle of New Orleans. His impressive equestrian statue stands prominently in the centre, symbolising the city's resilience. The surrounding buildings add to the historical ambiance: the grand St. Louis Cathedral and the Presbytère and Cabildo (now Louisiana State Museums) provide a window into the city's colonial past.

Jackson Square is a bustling centre of activity. Street artists display their colourful paintings and portraits, creating a vibrant atmosphere. Tarot card readers offer fortunes, and local musicians fill the air with traditional jazz tunes. The scent of freshly baked beignets from the famous Cafe Du Monde, located just across the street, entices visitors to indulge in New Orleans' culinary delights.

Jackson Square is the perfect starting point for further exploration. Horse-drawn carriages provide a charming way to tour the French Quarter, and the mighty Mississippi River flows just beyond the levee. You can stroll along the scenic riverfront or take a riverboat cruise for a unique view of the city skyline.

Tips for Your Visit

1. Timing: The square is lively all day, but arriving early in the morning allows for great photos without the crowds.
2. Bring Cash: Many street artists and local vendors accept only cash.
3. People Watching: Sit on a bench and soak in the vibrant atmosphere. Jackson Square offers a snapshot of New Orleans' diverse cultures and personalities.

4. Explore Further: Use Jackson Square as a starting point to delve deeper into the French Quarter's rich history and hidden gems.

* * *

The National WWII Museum

The National WWII Museum, originally called The National D-Day Museum, stands as a poignant tribute to the sacrifices of World War II. Designated by Congress as America's official National WWII Museum, it is a must-visit for history enthusiasts and anyone looking to understand this crucial period in history.

The museum provides an immersive experience, allowing visitors to step into the heart of the war. Through multimedia exhibits, personal stories, artefacts, and even a restored PT-boat, you'll gain a deep insight into the war's profound impact on soldiers, civilians, and the global landscape.

Highlights of the Museum
1. The Road to Berlin: This permanent exhibit outlines the key events of World War II, from the rise of Nazi Germany to the war's end. Interactive displays, personal narratives, and historical artefacts vividly bring the war to life.

2. D-Day Pavilion: Dedicated to the crucial D-Day invasion, this pavilion includes a meticulously recreated section of Omaha Beach, complete with sand, barbed wire, and landing craft. Artefacts and multimedia presentations convey the bravery and sacrifices of the Allied forces on that pivotal day.

3. Beyond the Battlefield: This exhibit goes beyond the frontlines, exploring civilian experiences on the home front, the significant contributions of women in the war effort, and the horrors of the Holocaust.

Experiences Beyond Exhibits

1. PT-305: Tour and even ride on this authentically restored PT-boat, an essential vessel from the war.

2. Personal Stories: Listen to recorded oral histories from veterans, civilians, and home front workers.

3. Special Exhibits: The museum frequently features temporary exhibits that explore specific aspects of World War II in greater detail.

Planning Your Visit

1. Location: Located in the heart of New Orleans on Andrew Higgins Drive, the museum is easily accessible by car, streetcar, or bus.

2. Tickets: Purchase tickets online or at the entrance. Multi-day passes are available if you plan to spend more time exploring.

3. Audio Tours: Enhance your visit with an audio tour, available in multiple languages.

4. Allow Enough Time: The museum is extensive, so plan to spend at least half a day to fully appreciate the exhibits.

* * *

Frenchmen Street

Frenchmen Street, a lively three-block stretch in the Faubourg Marigny neighbourhood, is the beating heart of New Orleans' live music scene. Once a well-kept secret among locals, it has become a must-visit destination for music enthusiasts from around the globe.

As you step onto Frenchmen Street, the vibrant sounds of live music greet you from every doorway. Unlike Bourbon Street, which is known for its mainstream party vibe, Frenchmen Street offers a diverse musical landscape. You'll find pulsating jazz clubs, soulful blues bars, energetic brass bands, and even Latin and reggae rhythms. Whatever your musical preference, Frenchmen Street has something to get your feet tapping.

Intimate Venues and Legendary Stages
   The charm of Frenchmen Street lies in its collection of intimate music venues. Historic spots like the Spotted Cat and Snug Harbor Jazz Bistro provide a close-up experience with world-class musicians. Venues such as d.b.a. (short for "dilettante barring association") and Apple Barrel buzz with energy, perfect for dancing the night away. Here, you can catch up-and-coming local talent or legendary musicians, making for an unforgettable experience.

Nightlife with Soul
   Beyond the music, Frenchmen Street offers a relaxed atmosphere ideal for enjoying a drink and soaking in the vibrant energy. Sit at a sidewalk cafe and watch as the street comes alive at night. Many venues have outdoor seating, allowing you to enjoy the music while sipping on a cocktail or local beer. The absence of flashing neon lights and raucous crowds makes for a more intimate and authentic nightlife experience.

While music is the main attraction, Frenchmen Street has more to offer. Several art galleries showcase local talent, and a variety of restaurants cater to hungry music fans. Whether you crave casual pub fare or upscale Creole cuisine, you'll find the perfect pre- or post-show meal to complement your musical adventure.

Tips for Experiencing Frenchmen Street

1. Arrive Early: Popular venues can get crowded, especially on weekends. Arrive early to secure a good spot or avoid waiting in line.

2. Cash is King: While some venues accept cards, many smaller clubs prefer cash. Bring enough to avoid any hassles.

3. Respect the Music: Remember, this is a place for musicians and music lovers. Be mindful of noise levels and conversations during performances. Show your appreciation by tipping the musicians.

4. Explore Different Venues: With so many options, don't limit yourself to one spot. Hop from venue to venue to discover the diverse musical offerings on Frenchmen Street.

* * *

The Garden District

The Garden District, nestled amidst the vibrant tapestry of New Orleans, is a tranquil haven offering a glimpse into the city's aristocratic past. Leave behind the lively French Quarter and find yourself immersed in a world of majestic mansions, meticulously tended gardens, and a timeless Southern allure.

Established in the early 19th century by affluent American immigrants seeking refinement, the Garden District thrived during the cotton boom. Wealthy merchants and plantation owners erected opulent mansions along broad, tree-lined streets like St. Charles Avenue, now an iconic landmark and a stop on the city's renowned streetcar line. From Greek Revival to Italianate, each mansion boasts intricate details and a sense of grandeur. Today, the Garden District proudly holds the title of a National Historic Landmark District, meticulously preserving its architectural legacy.

While the architecture steals the spotlight, the Garden District offers a wealth of experiences for visitors:

1. Lafayette Cemetery No. 1: Wander through a maze of above-ground tombs amidst lush surroundings. Known for its elaborate marble mausoleums and intricate sculptures, Lafayette Cemetery No. 1 provides insight into New Orleans' burial customs and cultural heritage through guided tours.

2. St. Charles Avenue Streetcar Ride: Embark on a nostalgic journey aboard the historic St. Charles Avenue streetcar. Glide past grand mansions, marvelling at their architectural splendour and soaking in the genteel ambiance. It's a quintessential New Orleans experience.

3. Lafayette Square: Nestled in the heart of the Garden District, Lafayette Square is a beloved green space. Relax beneath the shade of live oak trees, observe the locals, or engage in a leisurely game of chess.

4. Boutiques and Art Galleries: Bordering the Garden District, Magazine Street beckons with its array of boutiques, art galleries, and antique stores. Discover locally crafted treasures and regional artwork as you stroll along this charming thoroughfare.

5. Culinary Delights: The Garden District boasts a sophisticated culinary scene. From upscale dining establishments housed in historic mansions to cosy cafes serving brunch favourites, there's something to satisfy every palate.

Indulge in classic New Orleans fare like Po'Boys or fresh seafood at one of the neighbourhood's esteemed eateries.

Planning Your Visit

1. Explore the Garden District on foot or by bicycle to fully appreciate its architectural beauty and charming streetscapes.
2. Consider joining a guided walking tour to delve deeper into the neighbourhood's history and architecture.
3. While many mansions are private residences, some offer museum tours or limited access. Research these options beforehand if interested.
4. Respect the tranquillity of the neighbourhood and keep noise levels to a minimum out of consideration for local residents.

The Garden District is a captivating fusion of history, architecture, and Southern allure. Step back in time and relish the elegance of a bygone era in this enchanting New Orleans enclave.

* * *

A Swamp Tour

New Orleans offers more than just bustling streets and vibrant music. Venture beyond the city and explore a hidden world brimming with life on an exciting swamp tour. The swamplands surrounding New Orleans form a unique ecosystem, a mesmerising mosaic of cypress trees, winding waterways, and an array of captivating wildlife. A swamp tour provides an immersive experience that allows you to witness this natural wonder firsthand.

Gliding Through the Swamps

Swamp tours typically offer two main types of boats:

1. Flat-bottomed boats: These smaller vessels navigate narrow waterways, providing an intimate encounter with the swamp's inhabitants.

2. Airboats: Offering a thrilling high-speed ride, airboats skim across the water's surface, offering a panoramic view of the expansive ecosystem. They're ideal for covering a larger area and experiencing the excitement of gliding through the swamp.

Wildlife Encounters

Keep your eyes peeled for a diverse array of creatures that call the swamp home:

1. Alligators: These prehistoric reptiles, some reaching up to 13 feet in length, are the stars of the swamp. Your experienced guide will share intriguing facts about their behaviour and habitat.

2. Snakes: From non-venomous water snakes to the cottonmouth moccasin (listen to your guide's instructions!), be on the lookout for these slithering swamp residents.

3. Turtles: Whether basking on logs or gracefully swimming, turtles are a common sight in the swamp. Spot various species, including the alligator snapping turtle, with its prehistoric appearance.

4. Birds: The swamp is a paradise for birdwatchers, hosting egrets, herons, pelicans, and numerous other avian species, contributing to the symphony of sounds in the swamp.

5. Nutria: Often mistaken for beavers, these sizable, semi-aquatic rodents are another intriguing feature of the swamp.

A swamp tour offers more than just animal encounters. Your knowledgeable guide will shed light on the delicate balance of the swamp ecosystem, emphasising the importance of these wetlands and ongoing conservation efforts. You might also learn about the unique Cajun culture and its deep ties to the swamp environment.

Choosing a Tour

Consider the following factors when selecting a swamp tour:

1. Tour Duration: Choose a duration that aligns with your schedule and interests, typically ranging from 1.5 to 3 hours.

2. Boat Type: Decide between a flat-bottom boat for a more intimate experience or an airboat for an adrenaline rush.

3. Pick-up and Drop-off: Many companies offer convenient hotel pick-up and drop-off services in New Orleans.

4. Price: Prices vary based on duration, boat type, and included amenities. Shop around to find a tour that suits your budget.

Tips for Your Swamp Tour

1. Wear comfortable clothing and closed-toe shoes, with long pants recommended for protection.
2. Bring sunscreen, a hat, sunglasses, and insect repellent to shield against sun exposure and mosquitoes.
3. Don't forget your camera to capture breathtaking photos of the swamp scenery and wildlife encounters.

* * *

St. Louis Cathedral

Dominating the skyline of Jackson Square, the St. Louis Cathedral is not just a place of worship; it's a cornerstone of New Orleans' history and cultural fabric. As the oldest continuously operating cathedral in the United States, it symbolises the city's blend of French and Spanish influences.

Established in 1718, the initial church on this site was dedicated to King Louis IX of France, also known as Saint Louis. The current structure, finished in the mid-1800s, showcases a fusion of architectural styles, drawing from Spanish Colonial and Baroque influences. Its triple-steepled facade is an iconic feature of the New Orleans skyline.

The cathedral's interior is a testament to grandeur and artistry. High ceilings, intricate stained-glass windows portraying biblical tales, and ornate statues contribute to a reverential ambiance. Wander through the side chapels, each honouring different saints, and marvel at the magnificent pipe organ.

Throughout its existence, the St. Louis Cathedral has played a vital role in New Orleans' history. It has provided solace during crises like yellow fever outbreaks and Hurricane Katrina. It has also been a witness to joyous celebrations and significant events, including Pope John Paul II's visit in 1987.

Visitors are welcome to explore the cathedral during set hours, being mindful of ongoing services. Self-guided tours allow for a leisurely appreciation of the architecture and artwork. Daily masses offer a chance to partake in local traditions and connect with the city's spiritual core.

Planning Your Visit

CHAPTER 2: MUST-SEE ATTRACTIONS

1. Location: 615 Pere Antoine Alley, New Orleans, LA 70116 (French Quarter)
2. Hours: Open daily, with specific times for tours and services (check the official website for details).
3. Admission: Entry is free, with donations appreciated.
4. Dress Code: Modest attire is suggested during religious services.

* * *

City Park

New Orleans isn't just about lively streets and bustling crowds. Escape the urban energy and discover the tranquillity of City Park, a sprawling 1,300-acre urban oasis fondly known as the "green lung" of the city. Here, visitors of all ages and interests can find a diverse range of activities and attractions.

City Park offers a network of walking and jogging paths winding through lush greenery, perfect for nature enthusiasts. Rent bikes to explore the park's vast expanse at your leisure, or simply unwind on a park bench and soak in the peaceful atmosphere. Several scenic lagoons and waterways add to the park's allure, providing opportunities for leisurely paddle boat rides.

A Feast for the Eyes

1. New Orleans Museum of Art (NOMA): Immerse yourself in art history at NOMA, home to an impressive collection spanning centuries and continents. From European masterpieces to contemporary American works, the museum caters to diverse artistic tastes.

2. Besthoff Sculpture Garden: Adjacent to NOMA, explore the Besthoff Sculp-

ture Garden, an open-air sanctuary for contemporary sculptures. Wander amidst thought-provoking pieces and capture stunning photos against the vibrant New Orleans skyline.

3. Botanical Garden: Enter a world of botanical wonders at the New Orleans Botanical Garden. Explore themed gardens showcasing diverse plant life from around the world, including a vibrant rose garden, a tranquil Japanese garden, and a captivating swamp exhibit.

Family Fun for Everyone

1. Carousel Gardens Amusement Park: Take a nostalgic trip at Carousel Gardens Amusement Park, featuring classic rides like a carousel, a Ferris wheel, and a miniature train, perfect for entertaining younger visitors.

2. Storyland: Let imaginations run wild at Storyland, a whimsical playground featuring fairytale-themed structures and play areas where children can explore and create their own adventures.

3. City Putt: Challenge friends and family to a round of mini-golf at City Putt, offering fun for all ages.

City Park also offers numerous tennis courts, a golf course, a flying disc course, and a dog park for furry companions to roam freely. During cooler months, check the calendar for outdoor concerts and events, adding to the vibrant atmosphere.

History enthusiasts can explore the historic Couturie Forest, a remnant of the primaeval cypress swamp that once dominated the area. The 1854 New Orleans City Park Arboretum showcases a collection of mature live oak trees draped in Spanish moss, offering a glimpse into the city's natural heritage.

Tips for Your Visit

1. Plan your visit based on your interests, and grab a map online or at the park entrance.
2. Wear comfortable shoes for walking or biking.
3. Bring sunscreen, hats, and water, especially in warmer months.
4. Pack a picnic or enjoy food from vendors within the park.
5. City Park offers free on-site parking, though it can fill up on weekends. Consider alternative transportation like ride-sharing or biking.

* * *

Audubon Zoo and Aquarium of the Americas

New Orleans isn't just about vibrant streets and delicious food! Tucked within the city's urban landscape lies a paradise for animal lovers – the Audubon Zoo and Aquarium of the Americas, consistently recognized among the nation's top zoos and aquariums. This combined facility offers a unique chance to delve into the wonders of the animal kingdom, from the familiar to the exotic.

Audubon Zoo

Spanning over 50 acres, the Audubon Zoo whisks you away to diverse habitats worldwide. Explore the lush Louisiana Swamp, where iconic alligators, white pelicans, and otters reside. Encounter majestic Sumatran orangutans swinging through the trees in the acclaimed Asian Domain. Witness the playful antics of African penguins in their chilly habitat. The zoo also features exhibits like Jaguar Jungle, Elephant Exhibit, and Wings of the World, a free-flight aviary bustling with colourful birds.

Encounters and Experiences: Beyond animal viewing, the Audubon Zoo offers enriching experiences. Get hands-on with stingrays in the interactive touch tank or witness the intelligence of orangutans during a Wild Encounter (reservation required). Seasonal events and educational programs cater to visitors of all ages, adding fun and learning to the experience.

Aquarium of the Americas

Dive into the mesmerising underwater realm at the Aquarium of the Americas. Explore the Caribbean Reef, where colourful fish, graceful sea turtles, and impressive sharks glide through a massive 300,000-gallon tank. Journey through the Amazon Rainforest, encountering piranhas, anacondas, and a myriad of freshwater creatures. Discover the wonders of the Mississippi River and the Gulf of Mexico, meeting native fish, playful otters, and a captivating Louisiana white alligator.

More than just a showcase, the Aquarium of the Americas offers interactive exhibits highlighting conservation and marine ecosystems. Touch a stingray, witness a piranha feeding frenzy, or marvel at the ethereal beauty of jellyfish. Educational programs deepen understanding and appreciation for the underwater world.

Combined Admission and Tips

1. Both attractions are part of the Audubon Nature Institute. Purchasing a combined ticket grants access to both, ensuring a full day of exploration.
2. Arrive early, especially on weekends and holidays, to beat the crowds.
3. Comfortable shoes are a must, as both facilities require ample walking.
4. Protect yourself from the sun with sunscreen and a hat, especially in summer.
5. Bring water and snacks, though food options are available on-site.
6. Download the Audubon Nature Institute app for maps, animal info, and show schedules.

CHAPTER 2: MUST-SEE ATTRACTIONS

* * *

Café du Monde

Café du Monde stands as a New Orleans icon, as synonymous with the city as Mardi Gras beads and the soulful melodies of jazz. Since its establishment in 1862, this legendary open-air coffee stand has been delighting visitors with its steaming café au lait and fluffy beignets for over 160 years.

Stepping into Café du Monde is like stepping into the heart of New Orleans. The aroma of freshly brewed chicory coffee blends with the sweetness of powdered sugar adorning the beignets. The lively atmosphere, filled with chatter and laughter, adds to the vibrant experience that's as much about the ambiance as the delectable treats.

What to Savour

1. Café au Lait: The star attraction! Café du Monde's signature drink combines strong chicory coffee with steamed milk, creating a creamy, earthy blend. Served in a classic white ceramic cup, it's perfect for warming your hands on a chilly morning.

2. Beignets: These golden, square pastries are fried to perfection and generously dusted with powdered sugar. The contrast between the warm, fluffy interior and the crisp exterior is divine. Best shared with friends, diving into a plate of beignets is a messy but delightful experience!

Tips for Your Visit

1. Expect a Wait: Popular demand often means long lines, especially during peak times. Patience is key, or consider visiting during quieter hours.
2. Embrace the Ambiance:Seating may be limited, but the open-air setting

adds to the café's charm. Grab a seat at a communal table and soak in the lively atmosphere.

3. Cash Only: Café du Monde operates on a cash-only basis, so ensure you have bills on hand.
4. Explore Beyond the Classics: While café au lait and beignets steal the show, the menu offers other options like iced coffee and café noir. You can also purchase their coffee and beignet mix to recreate the experience at home.

Chapter 3: Culinary Delights and Cultural Experiences

Iconic New Orleans Dishes

New Orleans boasts a diverse culinary scene, reflecting its rich cultural tapestry. From savoury stews to succulent seafood and irresistible desserts, the city tantalises taste buds with an array of flavours. Here's a rundown of some quintessential New Orleans dishes, along with where to find them and their approximate prices:

1. Gumbo (Price Range: $15 - $30): This hearty stew, a staple of Creole cuisine, features a flavorful mix of roux, vegetables, and meat or seafood. For an authentic taste, try it at Arnaud's Restaurant or Dooky Chase's Restaurant.

2. Jambalaya (Price Range: $18 - $35): A flavorful one-pot dish combining rice, meat, and spices, with variations in Creole and Cajun styles. Coop's Place and Jacques-Imo's Cafe offer delicious renditions.

3. Po'Boy (Price Range: $12 - $20): A beloved New Orleans sandwich, packed with various fillings and served on French bread. Mother's Restaurant and Domilise's Po-Boy & Bar are renowned for their tasty po'boys.

4. Crawfish Étouffée (Price Range: $20 - $35): A luscious stew featuring

crawfish in a savoury sauce, typically served over rice. Brennan's Restaurant and Jacques-Imo's Cafe are top spots to savour this dish.

5. Red Beans and Rice (Price Range: $10 - $20): A classic Monday meal in New Orleans, consisting of red beans simmered with sausage and spices, served atop rice. Tiana's Po'Boys & Neighborhood Cafe and Li'l Dizzy's Cafe offer authentic versions.

6. Beignets (Price Range: $3 - $5 per order): Irresistible square pastries dusted with powdered sugar, best enjoyed fresh and warm. Café du Monde and Cafe Beignet are must-visit destinations for this iconic treat.

* * *

Best Restaurants and Cafes

New Orleans boasts a paradise for food enthusiasts, showcasing a lively culinary scene that mirrors its diverse cultural roots. From traditional Creole and Cajun delicacies to hip cafes and inventive eateries, the city caters to every taste and budget. Here's a handpicked selection of must-visit restaurants and cafes, along with their hours of operation, to tempt your palate.

Classics of New Orleans Cuisine

1. Brennan's: (French Quarter) Established in 1940, this historic gem offers an authentic fine dining experience with signature dishes like turtle soup and bananas Foster in a refined ambiance. Open: Lunch: Mon-Fri 11:30 am - 2:00 pm, Dinner: Daily 5:30 pm - 10:00 pm

2. Commander's Palace: (Garden District) Nestled in a Victorian mansion, in-

dulge in upscale Creole cuisine with their renowned tasting menus, promising a culinary journey like no other. Open: Lunch: Tues-Fri 11:30 am - 2:00 pm, Dinner: Tues-Sun 6:00 pm - 10:00 pm (Closed Mondays)

3. Dooky Chase's Restaurant: (Treme) A historic landmark celebrated for its soulful fare and Creole classics. Open: Tues-Sat 11:00 am - 8:00 pm (Closed Sundays and Mondays)

Relaxed Eateries and Cafes

1. Cafe Beignet: (Multiple Locations) Don't miss the chance to savour Café Beignets iconic experience with chicory coffee and beignets at various spots across the French Quarter. Open: Daily 24 hours

2. Cafe Du Monde: (French Quarter) The ultimate destination for beignets, offering a taste of authentic New Orleans tradition. Open: Daily 6:15 am - 11:00 pm

3. Rue Bourbon Beignets: (French Quarter) Putting a spin on the classic, Rue Bourbon Beignets features innovative flavours like chocolate chip or praline. Perfect for a quick sweet fix. Open: Daily 7:00 am - 10:00 pm

Contemporary Cuisine and Creative Flavours

1. Shaya: (Warehouse District) Led by acclaimed chef Alon Shaya, this restaurant delivers a modern interpretation of Israeli cuisine with Mediterranean influences. Open: Dinner: Sun-Thurs 5:30 pm - 10:00 pm, Fri & Sat 5:30 pm - 10:30 pm (Closed Mondays)

2. Compère Lapin: (Warehouse District) Pioneering innovative Creole dishes using seasonal ingredients, this spot has earned critical acclaim. Open: Dinner: Tues-Sun 5:30 pm - 10:00 pm (Closed Mondays)

3. Domenica: (Warehouse District) Offering lively Italian fare including housemade pasta and wood-fired pizzas. Open: Lunch: Mon-Fri 11:30 am - 2:30

pm, Dinner: Daily 5:00 pm - 10:00 pm

Exploring Beyond the French Quarter

1. Liuzza's Restaurant & Bar: (Mid-City) A casual setting for authentic New Orleans cuisine, renowned for its fried chicken and seafood gumbo. Open: Lunch: Mon-Fri 11:00 am - 2:30 pm, Dinner: Mon-Thurs 5:00 pm - 9:00 pm, Fri & Sat 5:00 pm – 10:00 pm (Closed Sundays)

2. Jacques-Imo's Cafe: (Treme) A local gem celebrated for its warm atmosphere and classic Creole dishes. Open: Tues-Thurs 11:00 am - 8:00 pm, Fri & Sat 11:00 am - 9:00 pm (Closed Sundays and Mondays)

3. Toups Meatery: (Mid-City) Starting as a butcher shop, this spot transforms into a vibrant eatery at night, serving up delectable Cajun fare with a focus on meats. Open: Dinner: Tues-Thurs 5:00 pm - 9:00 pm, Fri & Sat 5:00 pm - 10:00 pm (Closed Sundays and Mondays)

* * *

Local Traditions and Customs

New Orleans is a city steeped in tradition, where history and vibrant cultural practices blend seamlessly. Aside from the iconic Mardi Gras festivities, a myriad of unique customs and celebrations enhance the city's allure.

Here's a glimpse into some local traditions that will enrich your New Orleans experience:

1. Second Line Parades: Distinct from Mardi Gras parades, Second Line parades are jubilant processions that follow brass bands through the streets. These joyous events often occur after funerals, graduations, or social gatherings.

CHAPTER 3: CULINARY DELIGHTS AND CULTURAL EXPERIENCES

Everyone is welcome to join the parade, dancing and waving handkerchiefs to the infectious rhythms. Keep an eye out for colourful umbrellas and handkerchiefs, a traditional way to show your desire to participate.

2. Jazz Funerals: More than sombre affairs, New Orleans funerals are celebrations of life. After a traditional ceremony, a brass band leads a lively procession through the streets, playing mournful tunes en route to the cemetery and joyful music on the way back. This unique custom reflects the city's belief in the continuity of life beyond death.

3. Mardi Gras Indians: These elaborately attired African American social clubs are central to New Orleans culture. Their vibrant costumes, adorned with feathers and beads, pay homage to Native American traditions. Leading up to Mardi Gras, these groups perform traditional dances and chants, adding a unique dimension to the city's pre-Mardi Gras festivities.

4. Lagniappe (lan-yap): This charming custom embodies New Orleans' generous spirit. Lagniappe refers to a small extra something, an unexpected gift given by a merchant to a customer. It could be anything from an extra piece of candy to a discount on your purchase. Lagniappe serves as a reminder of the importance of community and the joy of giving.

5. Red Beans and Rice on Mondays: Originating from the tradition of soaking red beans on Sundays for a quick Monday meal, this culinary practice remains popular in New Orleans. Many restaurants feature red beans and rice on their Monday menus, often with flavorful additions like smoked sausage, tasso ham, or seafood.

6. Respecting the Traditions: While these traditions bring joy and cultural pride, it's crucial to show respect when encountering them. Avoid intruding on private events like funerals. If you join a Second Line parade, do so with enthusiasm while respecting the lead participants. By being mindful, you can fully appreciate the rich tapestry of New Orleans traditions.

NEW ORLEANS TRAVEL GUIDE 2024-2025

* * *

Festivals and Events

New Orleans is a city alive with celebration, where a vibrant array of festivals and events unfolds throughout the year, reflecting the city's rich cultural tapestry and infectious joie de vivre (joy of living).

Spring

1. Mardi Gras (February/March): The crown jewel of New Orleans festivals, Mardi Gras is a two-week extravaganza culminating on Fat Tuesday. Expect flamboyant parades, dazzling costumes, pulsating music, and an infectious spirit of revelry. (2024: February 13th, Fat Tuesday & 2025: March 4th, Fat Tuesday)

2. New Orleans Wine & Food Experience (May): A delightful journey through Louisiana's culinary landscape with tastings, celebrity chef demos, and cooking classes. (Mid-May for 2024 and 2025 dates to be confirmed)

3. New Orleans Jazz & Heritage Festival (April/May): A world-renowned celebration of jazz and diverse music genres over two weekends. (2024: April 25th to May 5th & 2025: Dates to be confirmed, typically late April/early May)

Summer

1. Essence Festival of Culture® Presented By Coca-Cola® (July): A celebration of African American art, music, and culture featuring renowned performers and inspirational speakers. (First weekend of July, dates for 2024 and 2025 to be confirmed)

2. Tales of the Cocktail (July): A week-long celebration of mixology with seminars, tastings, and competitions. (Late July, dates for 2024 and 2025 to

be confirmed)

3. Running of the Bulls (July): A quirky festival where participants outrun roller derby queens, inspired by the Spanish tradition. (Second Saturday of July, dates for 2024 and 2025 to be confirmed)

Fall

1. French Quarter Festival (April): A free three-day celebration of New Orleans' musical heritage. (Mid-April, 2025 dates to be confirmed)

2. Gentilly Fest (October): A family-friendly festival in the Gentilly neighbourhood with music, food vendors, and activities for all ages. (Second weekend of October, dates for 2024 and 2025 to be confirmed)

3. New Orleans Film Festival (October): A prestigious showcase of independent cinema and emerging filmmakers. (Mid-October, dates for 2024 and 2025 to be confirmed)

Winter

1. Bayou Bacchanal (November): A vibrant celebration of LGBTQ+ culture with music, dance, and parades. (First weekend of November, dates for 2024 and 2025 to be confirmed)

2. NOLA Christmas and New Year's Eve: Enjoy festive cheer and local flair with dazzling light displays, carolers in Jackson Square, and a lively New Year's Eve celebration.

This is just a taste of the multitude of festivals and events that fill the New Orleans calendar throughout the year.

Chapter 4: Accommodations in New Orleans

Rental Apartments

Please note that prices may vary depending on the season, availability, and amenities offered by each rental apartment. It's always a good idea to check for updated rates and availability before booking.

1. French Quarter Luxury Loft: Spacious loft apartment with modern amenities, located in the heart of the historic French Quarter. Features exposed brick walls, high ceilings, and a private balcony overlooking Bourbon Street.

- Location: French Quarter, New Orleans
- Price: $200-300 per night

2. Garden District Victorian Charm: Quaint Victorian-style apartment situated in the picturesque Garden District. Surrounded by tree-lined streets and historic homes, this cosy apartment offers a peaceful retreat with easy access to nearby cafes and shops.

- Location: Garden District, New Orleans
- Price: $150-250 per night

3. Marigny Musician's Hideaway: Eclectic apartment located in the vibrant Marigny neighbourhood, known for its lively music scene and colourful street art. This funky space features unique decor and is within walking distance of numerous bars and jazz clubs.

- Location: Marigny, New Orleans
- Price: $100-200 per night

4. Uptown Oasis with Balcony: Elegant apartment nestled in the historic Uptown district, offering a peaceful escape from the bustling city centre. Enjoy a spacious balcony overlooking tree-lined streets and easy access to nearby parks and attractions.

- Location: Uptown, New Orleans
- Price: $175-275 per night

5. Warehouse District Industrial Loft: Stylish loft apartment located in the trendy Warehouse District, known for its art galleries and trendy eateries. This industrial-chic space features exposed brick walls, high ceilings, and modern furnishings.

- Location: Warehouse District, New Orleans
- Price: $200-300 per night

6. Bywater Bohemian Retreat: Bohemian-style apartment situated in the eclectic Bywater neighbourhood, famous for its vibrant street art and hip cafes. This cosy retreat offers a laid-back atmosphere with easy access to local markets and live music venues.

- Location: Bywater, New Orleans

- Price: $125-225 per night

7. CBD Luxury High-Rise: Luxurious high-rise apartment located in the bustling Central Business District, offering panoramic views of the city skyline. Enjoy upscale amenities such as a rooftop pool, fitness centre, and concierge service.

- Location: CBD, New Orleans
- Price: $250-400 per night

8. Mid-City Historic Gem: Charming historic apartment located in the vibrant Mid-City neighbourhood, known for its diverse dining options and cultural attractions. This cosy gem features original hardwood floors, antique furnishings, and a serene courtyard.

- Location: Mid-City, New Orleans
- Price: $150-250 per night

9. Lakefront Retreat with Views: Tranquil lakefront apartment offering stunning views of Lake Pontchartrain. Located just a short drive from downtown New Orleans, this spacious retreat is perfect for nature lovers and outdoor enthusiasts.

- Location: Lakefront, New Orleans
- Price: $175-275 per night

10. Faubourg Marigny Artist Loft: Artist loft located in the vibrant Faubourg Marigny neighbourhood, known for its bohemian atmosphere and thriving arts scene. This unique space features exposed beams, hardwood floors, and

an inspiring creative vibe.

- Location: Faubourg Marigny, New Orleans
- Price: $125-225 per night

* * *

Hotels and Hostels

These accommodations cater to a range of budgets and preferences, providing options for both luxury seekers and budget-conscious travellers visiting New Orleans. Prices may vary depending on the season and availability.

1. The Ritz-Carlton, New Orleans: Located in the heart of the French Quarter, The Ritz-Carlton offers luxury accommodation with elegant rooms, fine dining options, and a full-service spa. It exudes Southern charm and hospitality.

- Location: 921 Canal St, New Orleans, LA 70112, USA
- Price per Night: Starting from $300 USD

2. Windsor Court Hotel: A sophisticated hotel known for its lavish décor and impeccable service. It features spacious rooms, a rooftop pool, award-winning restaurants, and a luxurious spa.

- Location: 300 Gravier St, New Orleans, LA 70130, USA
- Price per Night: Starting from $250 USD

3. Ace Hotel New Orleans: A trendy boutique hotel situated in a historic building in the Warehouse District. It offers stylish rooms, a rooftop pool and bar, live music events, and an on-site restaurant serving innovative cuisine.

- Location: 600 Carondelet St, New Orleans, LA 70130, USA
- Price per Night: Starting from $150 USD

4. International House Hotel: A boutique hotel with a chic, eclectic design located near the French Quarter. It features luxurious rooms, a renowned restaurant serving Creole cuisine, and a lively bar with craft cocktails.

- Location: 221 Camp St, New Orleans, LA 70130, USA
- Price per Night: Starting from $120 USD

5. The Pontchartrain Hotel: A historic hotel with a distinctive blend of old-world charm and modern amenities. Located in the Garden District, it offers elegant rooms, a rooftop bar with panoramic views, and a renowned restaurant.

- Location: 2031 St Charles Ave, New Orleans, LA 70130, USA
- Price per Night: Starting from $200 USD

6. HI New Orleans Hostel: A budget-friendly hostel located in a historic building in the Marigny neighbourhood. It offers dormitory-style and private rooms, a communal kitchen, social lounges, and organised tours and activities.

- Location: 1028 Canal St, New Orleans, LA 70112, USA
- Price per Night: Starting from $30 USD (dormitory) and $70 USD (private room)

7. India House Hostel: A laid-back hostel situated in a colourful Victorian mansion in Mid-City. It offers dormitory-style and private rooms, a communal kitchen, outdoor courtyard, and regular events like live music and BBQ nights.

- Location: 124 S Lopez St, New Orleans, LA 70119, USA
- Price per Night: Starting from $25 USD (dormitory) and $60 USD (private room)

8. St. Vincent's Guest House: A budget-friendly guesthouse housed in a former orphanage in the Lower Garden District. It offers simple yet comfortable accommodations, communal spaces, and easy access to nearby attractions.

- Location: 1507 Magazine St, New Orleans, LA 70130, USA
- Price per Night: Starting from $50 USD

9. The Quisby: A stylish boutique hostel located in a renovated historic building in the Lower Garden District. It offers dormitory-style and private rooms, a lively bar, communal kitchen, and social events.

- Location: 1225 St Charles Ave, New Orleans, LA 70130, USA
- Price per Night: Starting from $30 USD (dormitory) and $80 USD (private room)

10. Selina Catahoula New Orleans: A vibrant hostel located in a historic building in the Central Business District. It offers dormitory-style and private rooms, a rooftop terrace, co-working spaces, and a lively bar with live music and events.

- Location: 914 Union St, New Orleans, LA 70112, USA

- Price per Night: Starting from $40 USD (dormitory) and $100 USD (private room)

Chapter 5: Outdoor Activities and Recreation

Parks and Gardens

In New Orleans, it's not just about the lively streets and pulsating music scene. The city surprises with its abundance of parks and gardens, offering tranquil escapes for relaxation, discovery, and outdoor fun. Whether you fancy a peaceful walk amidst blooming flowers or a day of excitement with loved ones, New Orleans' parks and gardens cater to all.

Let's take a stroll through some highlights:

1. City Park: This sprawling 1,300-acre gem is the pride of New Orleans, featuring everything from serene gardens to thrilling amusement parks. Here are some must-see spots:

- New Orleans Botanical Garden: Lose yourself in a world of exotic plants from around the globe, meticulously displayed in curated gardens.
- Storyland: A whimsical wonderland for kids, filled with enchanting rides and fairytale-themed attractions.
- Carousel Gardens Amusement Park: Enjoy a nostalgic spin on the historic carousel or indulge in classic amusement park rides for the whole family.
- Sculpture Garden: Marvel at contemporary sculptures scattered through-

out the park, adding an artistic flair to the natural beauty.
- NOLA City Putt: Challenge your pals to a round of mini-golf on this playful 18-hole course.

2. French Quarter: Even amidst the bustling city centre, you'll find serene green spaces:

- Jackson Square: Escape the hustle and bustle amid this historic square, with the majestic St. Louis Cathedral as a stunning backdrop.
- Lalaland Park: A hidden oasis in the Treme neighbourhood, boasting lush greenery and a charming playground for a quick getaway.

Venture further out

1. Audubon Park: Located Uptown, this park offers tranquillity with its winding paths, scenic lagoon, and golf course. Plus, it's home to the Audubon Zoo and Aquarium of the Americas.

2. Bayou St. John: Nature lovers will delight in exploring this scenic waterway, perfect for kayaking, canoeing, and birdwatching amidst cypress swamps.

For an optimal experience

1. Pack a Picnic: Many parks have designated picnic spots, ideal for enjoying a leisurely meal surrounded by nature.
2. Rent a Bike: Explore City Park's vast expanse effortlessly on wheels, with bike rentals available near the park entrance.
3. Check for Events: Keep an eye out for concerts, farmers markets, or yoga sessions happening in the parks.
4. Sunscreen and Bug Spray: Shield yourself from the Louisiana sun and pesky mosquitoes with proper protection.

5. Respect the Environment: Help maintain the beauty of these spaces by disposing of trash responsibly and adhering to park rules.

New Orleans' parks and gardens offer a refreshing escape from the city's lively atmosphere, catering to diverse interests and providing a slice of nature's tranquillity. Whether you're seeking solitude, adventure, or quality time with loved ones, there's a green haven waiting to be explored.

***

Swamp Tours

New Orleans may boast a bustling urban scene, but just beyond its borders lies a world of wonder, the swamp. Embarking on a swamp tour promises an unforgettable adventure, immersing you in a realm teeming with intriguing wildlife and mystical allure.

Why opt for a swamp tour?

1. Encounter a Menagerie of Wildlife: Safely observe a myriad of creatures inhabiting the swamp, from sunbathing alligators to vibrant birds flitting amid the cypress trees, alongside turtles, snakes, and other critters.

2. Explore a Unique Habitat: Delve into the intricacies of the swamp's ecosystem, where freshwater meets saltwater. Your guide will illuminate the significance of this environment and its ecological role.

3. Experience the Thrill: Take your pick of excitement! Glide serenely through narrow waterways on a flat-bottomed boat, or feel the adrenaline surge on an

airboat adventure, skimming across the water's surface at thrilling speeds.

4. Delve into Local Lore: Many tours regale visitors with tales of swamp life, detailing traditional customs, fishing practices, and the symbiotic bond between humans and this remarkable landscape.

Types of Tours

1. Flat-bottomed Boat Excursions: Enjoy a quieter, more intimate journey, perfect for navigating narrow channels and getting up close to wildlife.

2. Airboat Adventures: Opt for a high-energy ride, offering exhilarating views of the expansive swamp as you zoom across the water.

Choosing Your Tour

Consider these factors when selecting your swamp expedition:

1. Duration: Tailor your tour to fit your schedule and interests, ranging from a few hours to a full day.

2. Activity Level: Decide between a leisurely flat-bottomed boat trip or the more exhilarating airboat experience.

3. Group Size: Choose between intimate outings or larger group adventures, depending on your preference for personalised attention.

4. Convenience: Look for tours offering hotel pick-up and drop-off services to streamline your experience.

5. Seasonal Considerations: While tours operate year-round, prime wildlife viewing is often during spring and fall.

Tips for Your Adventure

1. Dress for Comfort: Wear attire and footwear that can withstand potential wetness, especially on airboat rides.
2. Sun Protection: Shield yourself from the Louisiana sun with sunscreen, sunglasses, and a hat.
3. Bug Defence: Ward off mosquitoes with insect repellent, even during drier months.
4. Capture Memories: Bring a camera to immortalise the scenic beauty and wildlife encounters.
5. Respect Nature: Follow your guide's lead and refrain from disturbing the delicate ecosystem or its inhabitants.

* * *

Riverboat Cruises

The Mississippi River, a crucial lifeline of American commerce and history, is deeply woven into New Orleans' fabric. Embark on a scenic riverboat cruise to experience the Big Easy from a distinctive vantage point. These leisurely excursions blend sightseeing, history, and entertainment, making them ideal for visitors of all ages and interests.

Cruising Options

1. Daytime Sightseeing Cruises: These popular cruises, lasting 1-2 hours, offer stunning views of the city skyline, historic landmarks like Jackson Square and the French Quarter, and the bustling port activity along the river. Enjoy informative narration about the city's rich history and the Mississippi River's importance. Some daytime cruises also provide brunch or lunch options, perfect for combining sightseeing with a meal.

2. Dinner Cruises: Enhance your evening with a romantic dinner cruise. Glide along the Mississippi under the city's twinkling lights while savouring a multi-course meal. Live jazz music often accompanies these cruises, creating an unforgettable experience. Though pricier than daytime options, dinner cruises offer a luxurious way to experience New Orleans' vibrant nightlife.

3. Specialty Cruises: Several companies offer themed cruises for specific interests. These include historical cruises with detailed narration about events like the Battle of New Orleans or the city's architectural heritage. Sunset cruises provide a magical view as the skyline transforms into a kaleidoscope of colours. For a spooky twist, opt for a Halloween-themed cruise with costumed characters and eerie storytelling.

Choosing Your Riverboat Cruise

1. Consider Your Interests: Whether you want a relaxing sightseeing tour, a romantic dinner, or a themed adventure, choose an option that matches your preferences.

2. Time of Day: Daytime cruises offer stunning views and historical insights, while nighttime cruises provide a romantic ambiance with city lights.

3. Duration: Cruises range from short sightseeing tours to multi-hour dinner experiences. Select a timeframe that suits your schedule.

4. Budget: Daytime cruises are generally more affordable than dinner cruises. Specialty cruises may also come with a higher price tag. Consider additional costs like meals or drinks.

Tips for Your Riverboat Cruise

1. Book in Advance: Popular cruises, especially dinner cruises, can fill up quickly. Reserve your spot online or by phone to avoid disappointment.
2. Dress Code: Daytime cruises typically have a casual dress code, while

dinner cruises often recommend smart casual or cocktail attire. Check with the cruise operator for specifics.
3. Sun Protection: For daytime cruises, bring sunscreen and a hat to protect yourself from the sun.
4. Bring Your Camera: Capture stunning photos of the skyline, landmarks, and the Mississippi River.
5. Relax and Enjoy: Sit back, soak in the views, and let the gentle rhythm of the river enhance your experience.

* * *

Walking and Bike Tours

New Orleans is a city best experienced on foot or by bike. These modes of transportation let you truly immerse yourself in the vibrant neighbourhoods, captivating architecture, and hidden gems around every corner. Walking and bike tours are a fantastic way to explore the city, led by knowledgeable guides who share fascinating stories, historical insights, and local recommendations.

Walking Tours

Benefits

1. In-Depth Exploration: Walking tours let you delve deeper into specific areas like the French Quarter's rich history, the Garden District's architectural marvels, or the Faubourg Treme's vibrant jazz scene.

2. Hidden Gems: Local guides often know the hidden courtyards, quirky shops, and off-the-beaten-path attractions that independent travellers might miss.

3. Engaging Storytelling: Walking tours bring history to life with captivating narratives, anecdotes, and insights from passionate guides.

4. Flexibility: Many walking tours offer different themes and lengths to suit your interests and schedule. Some tours cater to specific interests like ghost stories, food, or architecture.

Types of Walking Tours

1. Historical Tours: Explore the French Quarter's colonial past, delve into the city's role in the Civil War, or learn about the impact of slavery on New Orleans' development.

2. Culinary Tours: Indulge your taste buds as you sample delicious local fare and learn about New Orleans' unique culinary heritage.

3. Ghost Tours: Embark on a spooky adventure through the city's haunted alleys and cemeteries, hearing chilling tales of the supernatural.

4. Neighborhood Tours: Dive deep into specific neighbourhoods like the Garden District, Faubourg Treme, or the Warehouse District, learning about their unique architecture, history, and cultural significance.

Bike Tours

Benefits

1. Cover More Ground: Bike tours allow you to explore a wider area of the city compared to walking tours, venturing beyond the French Quarter and into charming neighbourhoods like Treme or the Marigny.

2. Active Exploration: Enjoy a healthy and fun way to explore the city while getting some exercise.

3. Scenic Routes: Bike tours often take scenic routes along the Mississippi

Riverfront or through City Park, offering stunning views.

Types of Bike Tours

1. City Highlights Tours: Get a comprehensive overview of the city's major attractions, perfect for first-time visitors.

2. Food Tours: Combine your love of cycling with delicious food stops at local eateries and markets.

3. Swamp Tours: Embark on a unique adventure into the nearby swamps, exploring the ecosystem and spotting alligators and other wildlife from the safety of a bike path.

Choosing the Right Tour

1. Consider Your Interests: Do you want a historical deep dive, a spooky ghost tour, or a delicious culinary adventure?
2. Fitness Level: Walking tours are suitable for all fitness levels, while bike tours require some physical exertion.
3. Tour Duration: Choose from shorter tours for a quick introduction or longer tours for a more in-depth exploration.
4. Cost: Walking tours are generally cheaper than bike tours.

Chapter 6: Nightlife in New Orleans

Bars, Clubs and Live Music Venues

New Orleans overflows with music. From the soulful jazz tunes to the lively brass band rhythms, the city thrives on its vibrant nightlife. Whether you're in the mood for a chic cocktail bar, a dive bar with local legends, or an energetic dance club, New Orleans caters to all musical preferences and budgets. Here's a look at the diverse bars, clubs, and live music venues that keep the Big Easy alive.

Historic Haunts and Upscale Ambiance

French Quarter

1. Napoleon House: Step into history at this bar, rumoured to be haunted by Napoleon Bonaparte. Enjoy classic cocktails in a sophisticated setting. (Open daily from 11:00 AM to 3:00 AM, no cover charge)

2. Carousel Bar & Lounge: This iconic bar features a hand-carved carousel that slowly rotates while patrons enjoy expertly crafted cocktails. (Open daily from 11:30 AM to 3:00 AM, entry fee around $10 depending on the day and time)

Warehouse District

1. The Sazerac Bar at the Roosevelt New Orleans: Located in a historic hotel,

this bar is where the Sazerac, New Orleans' official cocktail, was born. Expect a refined atmosphere and top-notch service. (Open daily from 11:00 AM to 2:00 AM, no cover charge)

2. Cure: This award-winning cocktail bar is a haven for spirit enthusiasts, with bartenders crafting innovative cocktails using unique ingredients and techniques. (Open daily from 5:00 PM to 2:00 AM, no cover charge)

Live Music Hubs and Local Gems

French Quarter

1. Spotted Cat Music Club: An intimate jazz club showcasing local and emerging jazz talents, offering a genuine and electrifying experience. (Open daily from 2:00 PM to 2:00 AM, entry fee typically $10-$20)

2. Preservation Hall: A cornerstone of traditional jazz in New Orleans, this venue provides a lively atmosphere and the chance to see some of the city's best jazz musicians. (Open daily with multiple sets in the evening, entry fee typically $15-$20)

Faubourg Marigny

1. The Spotted Cat: Not to be confused with its French Quarter counterpart, this venue features a variety of live music from jazz to indie, with a spacious dance floor. (Open daily from 5:00 PM to 4:00 AM, entry fee typically $5-$10)

2. Three Muses: This vibrant bar has two stages featuring a mix of local jazz and indie acts. The delicious food menu makes it a great spot for dinner and a show. (Open daily from 11:00 AM to 3:00 AM, no cover charge during the week, cover charge on weekends)

Dance Clubs and Late-Night Hotspots

French Quarter

- Bourbon Street: Synonymous with New Orleans nightlife, this street is lined with bars and clubs, perfect for partygoers. Cover charges and drink prices vary widely by venue. (Most venues open until 4:00 AM)

Central Business District

- Republic NOLA: A massive nightclub with multiple dance floors and DJs spinning top hits, hip-hop, and EDM. It's a popular spot for a high-energy night out. (Open Fridays and Saturdays from 10:00 PM to 4:00 AM, entry fee typically $20-$30)

Tips for Navigating New Orleans' Nightlife

1. Do your research: Check online or local publications for upcoming events and performances.
2. Dress code: Most bars are casual, but some upscale places might have a dress code. Smart casual is a safe bet.
3. Cash is king: While many bars accept credit cards, having cash is handy, especially for smaller venues with minimal cover charges.
4. Pace yourself: Enjoy the vibrant nightlife responsibly and stay hydrated.
5. Stay aware: Keep your belongings close, particularly on Bourbon Street.
6. Embrace the vibe: New Orleans nightlife is about enjoying the music and letting loose. Put on your dancing shoes, grab a drink, and have fun!

Live music is the heart of New Orleans. From cosy jazz clubs to dynamic dance floors, the city offers a nightlife scene for every taste. By following these tips and exploring the venues, you can enjoy an unforgettable night out in the Big Easy.

CHAPTER 6: NIGHTLIFE IN NEW ORLEANS

* * *

Theatres and Performing Arts

New Orleans boasts a rich and vibrant theatre scene, offering a diverse range of productions beyond the infectious rhythms of live music venues. From historic playhouses showcasing Broadway classics to intimate stages presenting avant-garde performances, the city caters to all theatrical tastes.

Grand Dames and Historic Stages

1. The Saenger Theatre (French Quarter): This opulent theatre, a New Orleans landmark, is renowned for hosting touring Broadway productions, renowned musicians, and captivating ballets. Marvel at the stunning Beaux-Arts architecture and immerse yourself in the grandeur of a bygone era.

- Operation Hours: Box office hours are typically weekdays from 10:00 AM to 5:00 PM, showtimes vary depending on the production.
- Entry Fee: Ticket prices vary depending on the performance.

2. The Orpheum Theatre (Central Business District): Another architectural gem, the Orpheum Theatre offers a magnificent setting for Broadway musicals, concerts, and other live performances. The opulent interior and state-of-the-art acoustics create an unforgettable theatrical experience.

- Operation Hours: Box office hours typically weekdays from 10:00 AM to 5:00 PM, showtimes vary depending on the production.
- Entry Fee: Ticket prices vary depending on the performance.

Local Gems and Off-Beat Stages

1. Le Petit Theatre du Vieux Carré (French Quarter): This historic theatre, established in 1916, is the oldest continuously operating professional theatre company in the Southeast United States. They present a diverse season of productions, ranging from classic dramas to contemporary works.

- Operation Hours: Box office hours are typically weekdays from 12:00 PM to 5:00 PM, showtimes vary depending on the production.
- Entry Fee: Ticket prices vary depending on the performance.

2. The NOLA Project (Marigny): This innovative theatre company is known for its thought-provoking productions that explore contemporary social issues. They stage their performances in unique venues throughout the city, offering a fresh and dynamic theatrical experience.

- Operation Hours: Box office hours vary depending on the production, showtimes vary depending on the production.
- Entry Fee: Ticket prices vary depending on the performance.

Beyond the Stage

1. The Mahalia Jackson Theater of the Performing Arts (Central Business District): This modern performing arts centre hosts a variety of events, including Broadway shows, operas, ballets, and orchestral performances.

- Operation Hours: Box office hours are typically weekdays from 10:00 AM to 5:00 PM, showtimes vary depending on the production.
- Entry Fee: Ticket prices vary depending on the performance.

2. The Marigny Opera House (Faubourg Marigny): This non-profit arts organisation presents a unique blend of operatic, theatrical, and musical performances in a stunning 19th-century church setting.

- Operation Hours: Box office hours vary depending on the production, showtimes vary depending on the production.
- Entry Fee: Ticket prices vary depending on the performance.

Tips for Enjoying Theatre and Performing Arts in New Orleans

1. Purchase tickets in advance: Popular productions, particularly touring Broadway shows, can sell out quickly. Book your tickets online or through the theatre's box office well in advance.

2. Dress code: While most theatres don't have a strict dress code, opt for smart casual attire for most productions. For opening nights or galas, a more formal outfit might be appropriate.

3. Respect the performance: Turn off electronic devices and avoid disruptive behaviour during the show. Arrive early to find your seat and settle in before the performance begins.

Chapter 7: Shopping in New Orleans

Local Markets

New Orleans' vibrant culture extends beyond its music and festivals. The city boasts a network of bustling markets, offering a treasure trove of local produce, handcrafted goods, and unique souvenirs. Whether you're seeking fresh ingredients for a delicious meal, a one-of-a-kind piece of art, or a taste of local culture, these markets are a must-visit for any visitor.

French Quarter Marketplaces

1. French Market (French Quarter): This historic marketplace, located along the Mississippi River, is a sensory overload in the best way possible. Stroll through stalls overflowing with fresh produce, local seafood, and colourful flowers. Browse an array of local crafts, including handmade jewellery, artwork, and souvenirs.

- Operation Hours: Daily from 9:00 AM to 6:00 PM.

2. French Market Farmers Market (French Quarter): Held on Wednesdays and Sundays, this section of the French Market transforms into a paradise for food lovers. Local farmers showcase their seasonal bounty, offering fresh fruits, vegetables, herbs, and locally produced delicacies.

CHAPTER 7: SHOPPING IN NEW ORLEANS

- Operation Hours: Wednesdays and Sundays from 9:00 AM to 4:00 PM.

Beyond the French Quarter

1. Crescent City Farmers Market (Various Locations): This popular market rotates locations throughout the week, offering a chance to experience different neighbourhoods while shopping for fresh produce, artisan breads, locally raised meats, and handcrafted goods.

- Operation Hours: Varies depending on the location, typically Wednesdays and Saturdays from 9:00 AM to 1:00 PM. Check their website for the specific schedule.

2. Oak Street Poeyfarre Market (Faubourg Treme): This historic market, located in the Treme neighbourhood, offers a glimpse into local life. Find fresh produce, meats, and seafood alongside everyday household items and flowers.

- Operation Hours: Daily from 6:00 AM to 5:30 PM.

3. Magazine Street Market (Lower Garden District): Located on the vibrant Magazine Street, this market features a curated selection of local artisans selling handmade jewellery, clothing, artwork, and homeware.

- Operation Hours: Friday evenings from 5:00 PM to 9:00 PM and Sundays from 10:00 AM to 4:00 PM.

Tips for Exploring New Orleans' Markets

1. Bring Cash: While some vendors may accept credit cards, many prefer

cash. Having cash on hand ensures a smoother shopping experience.
2. Come Hungry: Many markets offer delicious food options, from fresh-baked bread to local specialties.
3. Haggling is Expected: In some markets, particularly for handmade crafts, haggling is an accepted part of the shopping experience.
4. Bring Your Reusable Bags: Many vendors are eco-conscious and encourage the use of reusable shopping bags.
5. Embrace the Atmosphere: Markets are a fantastic way to immerse yourself in the local culture and connect with friendly vendors.

* * *

Souvenir Shops

New Orleans is a treasure trove for souvenir hunters, with an abundance of shops catering to every taste and budget. Whether you seek Mardi Gras beads, voodoo dolls steeped in local lore, or quirky t-shirts proclaiming your love for the city, you'll find it all amongst the vibrant shelves of New Orleans' souvenir shops.

French Quarter Frenzy

The French Quarter is a shopper's paradise, with countless souvenir shops lining the bustling streets. Be prepared for a sensory overload as you browse through an array of colourful Mardi Gras paraphernalia, handcrafted jewellery, and artwork inspired by the city's unique culture.

- Typical Operation Hours: French Quarter shops generally operate extended hours to cater to tourists, with many staying open from 9:00 AM to 9:00 PM or even later, especially during peak seasons.

Beyond Bourbon Street

While Bourbon Street boasts a high concentration of souvenir shops, venturing beyond the main drag can unveil hidden gems. The Faubourg Marigny and the Warehouse District offer a more curated selection of boutiques with locally-made crafts and art.

Specialty Shops

1. Music Stores: Melomaniacs can delve into record stores specialising in jazz, blues, and other genres synonymous with New Orleans' musical heritage.
2. Antique Shops: Treasure hunters can unearth unique vintage finds and hidden antiques in shops scattered throughout the city.
3. Voodoo Shops: Immerse yourself in the city's mystical side by exploring shops selling voodoo dolls, gris-gris (protective charms), and other items associated with New Orleans' rich voodoo traditions. Remember, these items are often cultural objects, so approach with respect.

Tips for Souvenir Shopping in New Orleans

1. Haggling: While not as common as in other parts of the world, some negotiation might be possible, particularly at street vendors or shops with a large selection of similar items.

2. Support Local Artisans: Look for shops selling locally-made crafts and artwork to bring home a unique piece of New Orleans.

3. Compare Prices: Prices can vary between shops, so it's worth browsing a few stores before making a purchase.

4. Beware of Knock-Offs: Be cautious of low-quality knock-offs, especially on heavily touristed streets.

5. Embrace the Spirit: Souvenir shopping in New Orleans is about capturing the essence of the city. Choose items that resonate with you and will bring back cherished memories of your trip.

* * *

Art and Antique Stores

New Orleans pulsates with creativity. Beyond the infectious music and vibrant festivals, the city boasts a thriving art scene and a rich history of craftsmanship. Art and antique stores scattered throughout the city offer a treasure trove for collectors, enthusiasts, and anyone seeking a unique piece to commemorate their visit.

French Quarter Delights

1. Royal Street: This iconic street is a haven for art galleries and antique shops. Browse a diverse range of offerings, from contemporary paintings and sculptures to antique furniture and vintage jewellery. Many galleries participate in the monthly "Arts for All" events on the first Saturday of the month, offering extended hours and refreshments.

- Operation Hours: Varies by store, typically 10:00 AM to 5:00 PM, some open later on weekends

2. French Quarter Gallery (French Quarter): This established gallery showcases a curated collection of works by local and regional artists, encompassing various styles and mediums.

- Operation Hours: Daily from 10:00 AM to 6:00 PM

3. M.S. Rau (French Quarter): Covered in detail in Chapter 1 [refer readers to Chapter 1], this internationally renowned antique store offers a collection of high-end antiques, jewellery, and art, including originals by famed painters.

- Operation Hours: Wednesday to Tuesday from 9:00 AM to 5:15 PM, closed on Sundays

Beyond the French Quarter

1. Magazine Street: This charming street, lined with historic buildings and a mix of shops, also boasts a vibrant art scene. Discover galleries showcasing contemporary art, local crafts, and unique home décor items.

- Operation Hours: Varies by store, typically 10:00 AM to 5:00 PM, some open later on weekends

2. The Warehouse District: Converted warehouses in this district now house art galleries featuring a mix of established and emerging artists. Explore contemporary art installations, photography exhibits, and thought-provoking pieces.

- Operation Hours: Varies by store, typically Tuesday to Saturday from 11:00 AM to 5:00 PM

3. Oak Street: Located in the Uptown neighbourhood, Oak Street offers a more local art scene with galleries featuring works by up-and-coming artists and showcasing a variety of styles.

- Operation Hours: Varies by store, typically Wednesday to Saturday from 11:00 AM to 5:00 PM

Tips for Exploring Art and Antique Stores in New Orleans

1. Do your research: If you have specific interests, research galleries or antique shops known for those specialties before your visit.
2. Embrace the local flavour: Look for galleries showcasing works by local New Orleans artists. You might discover a unique piece that captures the city's spirit.
3. Haggling is acceptable: In some antique stores, particularly on Magazine Street, negotiation is part of the experience. Don't be afraid to make a reasonable offer.
4. Take your time: Art and antique browsing is best done at a leisurely pace. Wander through the stores, admire the works on display, and don't be afraid to ask questions from the gallery owners or staff. They are often passionate about the art and knowledgeable about the history of the pieces.

Chapter 8: Day Trips and Excursions

Plantations

New Orleans' history is deeply intertwined with its plantations, grand estates that once thrived on slave labour to cultivate extensive sugarcane fields. Though the legacy of slavery is a dark chapter, these historic sites provide insights into the antebellum South, its architecture, and its complex social and economic fabric. Today, many plantations operate as museums, educating visitors about the lives of both the plantation owners and the enslaved people.

Plantations near New Orleans offer diverse experiences. Some highlight the architectural splendour and the opulent lifestyles of the plantation owners, while others focus on the harsh realities of slavery and its impact on those who were enslaved.

When visiting, it's important to approach with respect and a willingness to learn about this complex history. Many plantations offer guided tours led by knowledgeable guides who provide informative and sensitive insights.

Popular Plantations near New Orleans

1. Oak Alley Plantation (Vacherie): Famous for its stunning avenue of ancient oak trees, Oak Alley offers tours of the restored mansion and explores the lives of both enslaved individuals and free people of colour who lived and worked

there. (Hours: Daily from 9:00 AM to 5:00 PM, Entry Fee: Varies by tour options)

2. Whitney Plantation (Wallace): Focused on interpreting slavery from the perspective of the enslaved, Whitney Plantation provides a powerful and unique experience. Tours cover the slave quarters, honour those who suffered, and celebrate the resilience of the African American community. (Hours: Daily from 9:00 AM to 5:00 PM, Entry Fee: Varies by tour options)

3. Laura Plantation (Vacherie): This well-preserved Creole plantation offers a look into the lives of a wealthy Creole family in the 19th century. Tours feature opulent furnishings and architecture while also recognizing the enslaved individuals who laboured there. (Hours: Daily from 9:00 AM to 5:00 PM, Entry Fee: Varies by tour options)

4 Houmas House Plantation and Gardens (Destrehan): This grand estate boasts beautiful gardens, a restored mansion, and swamp tours. While the focus is on the luxurious lifestyle of the plantation owners, the history of slavery is also addressed in the tours. (Hours: Daily from 9:00 AM to 5:00 PM, Entry Fee: Varies by tour options)

Tips for Visiting Plantations

1. Plan Your Visit: Check plantation websites for tour schedules, ticket prices, and special events. Booking tours in advance is recommended, especially during peak seasons.
2. Wear Comfortable Shoes: Many tours involve walking through the grounds and historic structures.
3. Be Respectful: These sites represent a complex and often painful history. Dress modestly and be mindful of your behaviour during your visit.
4. Ask Questions: Engaging with knowledgeable guides can enhance your understanding of the plantation's history.

CHAPTER 8: DAY TRIPS AND EXCURSIONS

✳ ✳ ✳

Nearby Cities and Towns

New Orleans is an enchanting city, but Louisiana offers a wealth of experiences beyond the allure of the French Quarter. For those eager to explore Cajun culture, historic plantations, or nature retreats, nearby cities and towns provide a rewarding adventure. Here are some intriguing options, all within a reasonable driving distance from New Orleans.

Immerse Yourself in Cajun Country

1. Lafayette (130 miles southwest): Known as the heart of Cajun Country, Lafayette features a vibrant cultural scene, delicious Cajun cuisine, and plenty of opportunities to experience the region's unique traditions. Visit Vermilionville, a historic village showcasing Cajun architecture and heritage crafts. Explore Acadian Village, a living history museum with costumed interpreters demonstrating traditional Cajun life. Savour a plate of crawfish étouffée or gumbo at one of Lafayette's many renowned restaurants, and don't miss the live Cajun and Zydeco music.

2. Breaux Bridge (100 miles southwest): Dubbed "The Crawfish Capital of the World," Breaux Bridge is a charming town rich in Cajun culture. Visit during the Crawfish Festival in the spring for a lively celebration of this Louisiana delicacy. Stroll down Main Street, lined with colourful shops and restaurants, and soak in the town's relaxed atmosphere. Take a swamp tour to see alligators and other wildlife in their natural habitat.

Step Back in Time at Historic Plantations

1. Oak Alley Plantation (30 miles west): This magnificent antebellum mansion, with its dramatic avenue of ancient oak trees, offers a glimpse into the grandeur of the antebellum South. Take a guided tour of the meticulously

restored plantation house and learn about the lives of the wealthy family who once owned it and the enslaved people who lived and worked there. Explore the serene grounds and appreciate the beauty of Southern plantation architecture.

2. Destrehan Plantation (25 miles west): Another stunning example of antebellum architecture, Destrehan Plantation features a unique raised French Creole cottage design. Tours cover the plantation's history, from its indigo and sugar production past to its role as a free home for formerly enslaved people after the Civil War. Wander through the lush gardens and admire the moss-draped live oak trees.

Embrace the Beauty of Nature

1. Jean Lafitte National Historical Park and Preserve (30 miles south): Escape the city and explore the wetlands and bayous of this national park. Take a swamp tour to see alligators, birds, and other wildlife in their natural habitat. Hike or bike along scenic trails, or rent a kayak to explore the waterways at your own pace. Learn about the unique ecosystem of the Mississippi Delta and its vital role in the environment.

2. Grand Isle (70 miles south): For a beach getaway, head to Grand Isle, a barrier island known for its sugar-white sand and calm waters. Relax on the beach, go swimming or fishing in the Gulf of Mexico, or try your hand at shelling. Enjoy a fresh seafood meal at a local restaurant and soak in the laid-back island atmosphere.

Planning Your Excursion

1. Consider your interests: Whether you crave cultural immersion, historical exploration, or a nature escape, choose your destination based on your preferences.
2. Factor in travel time: The distances listed are approximate driving times. Allow additional time for traffic and potential stops along the way.
3. Check seasonal offerings: Some festivals and events occur at specific

times of the year. Research events of interest beforehand to plan your trip accordingly.

* * *

Coastal Adventures

New Orleans' magic extends far beyond its city limits. The surrounding wetlands, swamps, and barrier islands offer a chance to experience Louisiana's unique ecosystem, teeming with diverse wildlife and rich in history and culture. Embark on a coastal adventure and discover a different side of Louisiana, from swamp tours encountering alligators to airboat rides exploring hidden bayous.

Swamp Tours

Experience: Glide through cypress swamps in a comfortable tour boat, led by knowledgeable guides who share fascinating insights about the ecosystem, local flora and fauna, and the history of the wetlands. Spot alligators basking in the sun, turtles perched on logs, and a variety of bird species soaring through the lush canopy.

Options

1. Half-Day Tours: Perfect for a quick introduction to the swamp ecosystem, these tours typically last 2-3 hours and explore areas closest to the city.

2. Full-Day Tours: Delve deeper into the swamps with a full-day adventure, venturing further out and offering a higher chance of encountering wildlife. Some tours even include lunch at a plantation or a local restaurant.

3. Swamp Walks & Photography Tours: For a more immersive experience, opt for a guided swamp walk where you can explore the ecosystem on foot along elevated boardwalks. Photography tours cater to shutterbugs, offering guidance on capturing stunning images of the swamps and their inhabitants.

Tips

1. Wear comfortable clothing and shoes: Long pants, closed-toe shoes, and insect repellent are recommended.
2. Bring sunscreen and a hat: The sun can be strong, especially on a boat with limited shade.
3. Be mindful of the wildlife: Maintain a safe distance from alligators and other animals and avoid disturbing their habitat.

Airboat Adventures

Experience: Feel the thrill of skimming across the water on a high-speed airboat. These tours venture into the heart of the swamps, offering an adrenaline-pumping adventure with stunning views of the vast wetlands. Hold on tight and enjoy the cool spray as you navigate through hidden bayous and discover the unique beauty of the Louisiana landscape.

Options

1. Narrated Tours: Learn about the swamps and their inhabitants from experienced guides who share interesting facts and stories throughout the airboat ride.

2. Sunset Tours: Witness the breathtaking beauty of a Louisiana sunset as you glide through the swamps, creating a truly unforgettable experience.

3. Fishing Charters: Combine your airboat adventure with a fishing expedition, targeting species like bass, catfish, and redfish in the swamp's hidden waterways.

CHAPTER 8: DAY TRIPS AND EXCURSIONS

Tips

1. Dress for the elements: Bring layers as it can be cooler on the water, especially in the mornings and evenings.
2. Ear protection: The airboat engines can be loud, so consider bringing earplugs or noise-cancelling headphones.
3. Secure your belongings: The airboat ride can be bumpy, so ensure your belongings are secure.

Plantation Tours

Experience: Step back in time and explore historic plantations that offer a glimpse into Louisiana's antebellum past. Learn about the history of these grand estates, the lives of the plantation owners and enslaved people, and the unique architectural styles. Some plantations offer beautiful gardens to explore and even showcase traditional Southern cuisine.

Options

1. Guided Tours: Choose a guided tour led by knowledgeable staff who can provide historical context and answer your questions.

2. Self-Guided Tours: Explore the plantation grounds and mansion at your own pace, with informative exhibits and signage providing historical details.

3. Combination Tours: Combine your plantation visit with a swamp or airboat tour for a well-rounded experience that explores Louisiana's history and ecosystem.

Tips

1. Research plantations before your visit: Some plantations focus more on the architectural aspects, while others delve deeper into the social and cultural history. Choose one that aligns with your interests.

2. Be respectful: Plantations represent a complex and often dark chapter in American history. Be mindful of the historical significance and approach your visit with respect.

Chapter 9: Planning Your Itinerary

A 7-Day General Itinerary

New Orleans offers an intoxicating blend of history, culture, music, and vibrant energy. This 7-day itinerary provides a framework to experience the city's highlights, leaving room for flexibility and personal exploration. Adapt it to suit your interests and pace, and get ready to be swept away by the magic of the Big Easy.

Day 1: Immerse Yourself in the French Quarter

- Morning: Start your day with a quintessential New Orleans breakfast of beignets and café au lait at Cafe du Monde in the heart of the French Quarter. Soak in the lively atmosphere and the city's unique charm.

- Afternoon: Explore the maze-like streets of the French Quarter, browsing art galleries on Royal Street, admiring the historic architecture of Jackson Square, and wandering through the bustling French Market for local crafts and souvenirs.

- Evening: Catch a free outdoor concert in Jackson Square, enjoy a jazz performance at a Frenchmen Street club, or take a voodoo-themed walking tour to delve into the city's mystical side.

Day 2: Unveiling History and Culture

- Morning: Visit the National World War II Museum to learn about the pivotal role New Orleans played in the war effort. Interactive exhibits and personal stories bring history to life.

- Afternoon: Take a streetcar ride on the iconic St. Charles Avenue, lined with grand mansions, and explore the Lafayette Cemetery No. 1, one of the city's oldest above-ground cemeteries, with a guided tour.

- Evening: Enjoy a traditional Creole dinner at a renowned restaurant in the French Quarter, followed by a lively jazz performance at a club on Frenchmen Street.

Day 3: A Day Beyond the City Limits

- Morning: Embark on a swamp tour through the nearby wetlands. Glide through cypress forests, spot alligators and other wildlife, and learn about the unique ecosystem from knowledgeable guides.

- Afternoon: Explore Oak Alley Plantation, a stunning antebellum mansion with rows of majestic oak trees lining the driveway. Learn about the plantation's history and take a walk through the beautiful gardens.

Day 4: Festival Fun (Adjust based on actual festival dates)

- Day: Immerse yourself in the vibrant energy of a New Orleans festival! Depending on the time of year, you might experience the electrifying atmosphere of Mardi Gras, the soulful sounds of the New Orleans Jazz & Heritage Festival, or the lively celebration of the Essence Festival.

Day 5: Explore Diverse Neighbourhoods

- Morning: Venture beyond the French Quarter and explore the Faubourg Marigny, a bohemian neighbourhood with colourful shotgun houses, art galleries, and trendy restaurants.

- Afternoon: Head to the Warehouse District, a hub of converted warehouses now housing art galleries, contemporary museums, and upscale boutiques. Explore the Ogden Museum of Southern Art or take a stroll along the Mississippi River waterfront.

- Evening: Catch a live music performance at a venue on Frenchmen Street in the Faubourg Marigny, offering a diverse range of musical styles from jazz and blues to funk and indie.

Day 6: Culinary Delights and Local Haunts

- Morning: Indulge in a delicious brunch at a local cafe in the French Quarter, followed by a cooking class to learn how to prepare classic New Orleans dishes like gumbo or jambalaya.

- Afternoon: Take a walking food tour through the Treme neighbourhood, the birthplace of jazz, sampling delicious local fare and learning about the neighbourhood's rich history and cultural significance.

- Evening: Embark on a ghost tour through the French Quarter, hearing spooky tales of the city's haunted past and exploring its atmospheric alleys and cemeteries.

Day 7: Farewell to the Big Easy

- Morning: Do some last-minute souvenir shopping on Magazine Street, a charming avenue lined with shops, cafes, and antique stores.

- Afternoon: Enjoy a final stroll through the French Quarter, soaking in the sights and sounds one last time before departing New Orleans. Reflect on the unforgettable experiences and the city's infectious joie de vivre (joy of living).

This itinerary offers a taste of the captivating experiences that await you in New Orleans. Remember, this is just a starting point! Feel free to adjust it based on your interests, energy level, and the festivals happening during your visit. Embrace the spontaneity, get lost in the vibrant atmosphere, and let the Big Easy work its magic on you.

* * *

A 3-Day Romantic Itinerary for Couples

New Orleans, with its infectious charm, captivating music, and vibrant culture, is the perfect city for a romantic getaway. This 3-day itinerary offers a mix of iconic experiences, hidden gems, and opportunities to create unforgettable memories together.

Day 1: Immersing Yourselves in the City's Soul

- Morning: Start your day with a leisurely stroll through the French Quarter. Admire the beautiful architecture, browse through unique shops on Royal Street, and fuel up with a delicious beignet and cafe au lait at a historic cafe like Cafe du Monde.

- Afternoon: Embark on a romantic carriage ride through the French Quarter. Let the clip-clop of the horses and the gentle breeze carry you past charming courtyards and historic landmarks as your guide shares stories about the city's rich past.

- Evening: Enjoy an intimate dinner at a candlelit restaurant in the French Quarter. Savour the flavours of New Orleans cuisine, with options ranging from classic Creole dishes to upscale French fare. End the evening with a jazz performance at a cosy club like Snug Harbor or Fritzel's Jazz Bar, letting the soulful melodies set the mood for a romantic night.

Day 2: Exploring Beyond the French Quarter

- Morning: Take a bike tour through the Garden District, admiring the stunning antebellum mansions and lush green spaces. Learn about the history of this iconic neighbourhood and its famous residents.

- Afternoon: Pack a picnic basket and head to City Park. Rent paddle boats and explore the scenic lagoons, or simply relax under the shade of a majestic oak tree and enjoy each other's company. In the afternoon, visit the New Orleans Museum of Art for a dose of culture, or explore the unique exhibits at the Audubon Aquarium of the Americas.

- Evening: Take a romantic cruise on the Mississippi River at sunset. Witness the breathtaking panorama of the city skyline as the sun dips below the horizon, creating a magical atmosphere. Enjoy a delicious dinner on board or simply share a bottle of wine and soak up the beauty of the moment.

Day 3: Unveiling Hidden Gems and Local Flavour

- Morning: Indulge in a decadent brunch at a local favourite like Cafe Beignet or Mother's Restaurant. People-watch on the bustling streets of the French Quarter and savour the delicious flavours of New Orleans' brunch scene.

- Afternoon: Venture to Faubourg Marigny, a charming neighbourhood known for its colourful shotgun houses, vibrant art scene, and lively bars. Explore the quirky shops along Frenchmen Street, and perhaps stumble upon a live music performance at one of the many local venues.

- Evening: Enjoy a cooking class together and learn how to prepare classic New Orleans dishes like gumbo, jambalaya, or po'boys. Bond over the experience of creating a delicious meal together, and then savour the fruits of your labour with a romantic dinner at home.

Romantic Touches

1. Pack a small picnic basket: Fill it with local cheese, bread, fruits, and a bottle of wine for a spontaneous picnic in one of the city's many parks.
2. Leave love notes around your hotel room: Surprise your partner with hidden messages expressing your love and appreciation.
3. Take a couples massage: Relax and unwind together at a spa, indulging in a pampering massage treatment.
4. Personalise your experience: Research unique experiences offered by local vendors, like a private swamp tour for two or a couples' painting class.

* * *

A 5-Day Culinary Itinerary

New Orleans' vibrant culinary scene offers a tantalising mix of iconic eateries, hidden gems, and diverse flavours. This 5-day itinerary will guide you through a delicious adventure that captures the essence of New Orleans cuisine.

Day 1: A Taste of Tradition

- Breakfast: Begin with a classic beignet at Café du Monde in the French Quarter. These fluffy fried pastries, dusted with powdered sugar, are a quintessential New Orleans breakfast.

- Lunch: Enjoy the French Quarter's atmosphere with lunch at Acme Oyster House. Savour a dozen freshly shucked oysters or a plate of their signature seafood gumbo.

- Dinner: Experience Creole elegance at Commander's Palace in the Garden District. Indulge in refined dishes featuring fresh, seasonal ingredients, such as turtle soup and blackened redfish.

Day 2: Exploring Local Gems

- Breakfast: Head to Magazine Street for breakfast at Rue St. Ferdinand. This lively spot offers delicious brunch options like fluffy pancakes and savoury eggs Benedict.

- Lunch: In the Faubourg Marigny, enjoy a po'boy lunch at Parkway Bakery & Tavern. These legendary sandwiches, piled high with meats and perfectly dressed, are a local staple.

- Dinner: Savour authentic Vietnamese cuisine at Dong Phuong Bakery in the Treme neighbourhood. Their renowned banh mi sandwiches, filled with savoury meats and pickled vegetables, are a must-try.

Day 3: A Celebration of Seafood

- Breakfast: Fuel up with a hearty breakfast at Mother's Restaurant, known for its variety of options including omelettes, pancakes, and their signature "debris" breakfast po'boy.

- Lunch: Enjoy a casual lunch at the New Orleans Fish House Market in the French Quarter. Choose from fresh seafood options like shrimp, oysters, and crawfish, prepared boiled, grilled, or fried.

- Dinner: Experience a lively New Orleans boil at Cochon Butcher in the Warehouse District. Gather around a communal table for a spread of boiled seafood, corn, potatoes, and sausage, seasoned to perfection.

Day 4: International Flavors

- Breakfast: Savour Central American flavours at Café NOLA in the Warehouse District, with dishes like huevos rancheros and breakfast burritos.

- Lunch: Enjoy comforting soul food at Dooky Chase's Restaurant in Treme, known for its historical significance and dishes like fried chicken, jambalaya, and red beans and rice.

- Dinner: Indulge in Italian cuisine at Adolfo's Restaurant in the Warehouse District. Enjoy classic dishes such as pasta, pizza, and veal parmesan.

Day 5: Sweet Endings and Local Favourites

- Breakfast: Indulge in a sweet breakfast at Cafe Beignet in Mid-City. Try a variety of beignets, including creative flavours like chocolate chip or praline.

- Lunch: Taste the iconic muffuletta sandwich at Central Grocery in the French Quarter. This unique sandwich, with Italian meats, cheeses, and olive salad on a sesame seed loaf, is a must-try.

- Dinner: End your culinary journey with a celebratory dinner at Brennan's of New Orleans in the French Quarter. Enjoy a fine-dining experience

CHAPTER 9: PLANNING YOUR ITINERARY

focused on classic Creole cuisine and impeccable service.

This itinerary is just the beginning. New Orleans is brimming with culinary experiences waiting to be discovered. Explore local farmers markets, sample street food from vendors, and try iconic New Orleans cocktails like the Sazerac and the Hurricane.

Chapter 10: Practical Information and Tips

Language and Communication

New Orleans is a city rich in cultural diversity, evident in its distinctive language and communication styles. Grasping these subtleties can enhance your experience and help you engage effectively with locals.

English: As the official language of the United States, English is predominantly spoken in New Orleans. However, you might notice some unique regional variations in pronunciation and vocabulary.

French: The historical connection to France is clear, especially with some residents, particularly older generations and those in the French Quarter, who might use French greetings or phrases, although English remains more common.

Louisiana Creole: This unique language, born from French, Spanish, and African influences, is spoken by a smaller group, primarily within Creole communities of colour.

Spanish: Given its closeness to Latin America and a growing Hispanic community, Spanish is increasingly spoken in New Orleans.

CHAPTER 10: PRACTICAL INFORMATION AND TIPS

Understanding the Local Expressions

- Y'all: This common Southern term for "you all" is widely used in New Orleans.
- Lagniappe (lan-yap): Means a little something extra, often referring to a bonus or an unexpected treat.
- Laissez les bons temps rouler (lay-zay lay bon tom roo-lay): Let the good times roll! This phrase embodies the city's celebratory spirit.
- Pack: In New Orleans, this can refer to having a good time or a large gathering, not just luggage.
- Nawlins: A colloquial term for New Orleans, frequently used by locals.

Communication Tips

1. Be patient: The pace of life here can be slower. Enjoy the conversation and feel free to ask for clarification if needed.
2. Embrace the accent: The distinct New Orleans accent is both charming and musical. Listen carefully and don't hesitate to ask someone to repeat themselves if you're unsure.
3. Southern hospitality is real: Locals are known for their friendliness and welcoming nature. Politeness and respect will often be met with warmth and helpfulness.
4. Learn a few basic French phrases: Simple greetings like "bonjour" (hello) or "merci" (thank you) can show respect for the city's French heritage.

* * *

Currency and Money Matters

Understanding how to handle currency exchange, tipping etiquette, and payment methods will ensure a smooth financial experience during your visit to New Orleans. Here's a concise guide to help you navigate these aspects.

Currency

The official currency in New Orleans, as in the rest of the United States, is the US Dollar (USD). Bills are available in $1, $5, $10, $20, $50, and $100 denominations. Coins come in $1 (dollar), $0.50 (fifty cents), $0.25 (quarter), $0.10 (dime), $0.05 (nickel), and $0.01 (penny).

Traveler's Checks

Though less common now, traveller's checks can still be exchanged for cash at banks or larger hotels. However, ATMs often offer better exchange rates.

Currency Exchange

If you need to exchange foreign currency for USD, you can do so at the airport or at exchange booths in the French Quarter. Banks generally offer better rates but may have limited hours and require identification.

Credit Cards and ATMs

Major credit cards like Visa, Mastercard, and American Express are widely accepted across New Orleans, including in restaurants, shops, hotels, and attractions. However, some smaller businesses or street vendors may only accept cash.

- ATMs: These are easily found throughout the city, allowing you to withdraw cash with your debit card. Check with your bank about any international transaction fees that may apply.

- Using Your Credit Card Abroad: Notify your bank of your travel plans to prevent any holds on your account due to suspected fraudulent activity.

Tipping Etiquette

Tipping is a customary practice in the United States. Here are the standard tipping rates:

1. Restaurants: 15-20% of the bill before tax for good service.
2. Bars: $1-$2 per drink.
3. Taxis: 10-15% of the fare.
4. Hotel Staff: $1-$5 per bag for bellhops and a small daily tip for housekeeping.

Always check your bill, as some restaurants may automatically include gratuity, especially for larger parties.

Additional Money-Saving Tips

1. Purchase a City Pass: This can provide discounted admission to popular attractions and save on sightseeing costs.

2. Free Activities: Enjoy free activities like exploring the French Quarter, attending outdoor concerts, or walking through City Park.

3. Public Transportation: Utilise the city's streetcars and buses for a convenient and affordable way to get around.

4. Pack a Water Bottle: Bring a reusable water bottle to stay hydrated and save on the cost of bottled water, especially at tourist spots.

By following these tips and planning your budget, you can enjoy a financially stress-free visit to New Orleans. Now, you're ready to dive into the Big Easy and enjoy its unique culture, rich history, and delicious cuisine.

* * *

Health and Safety Tips

New Orleans is a vibrant city full of life, culture, and memorable experiences. To ensure a smooth and enjoyable visit, consider these health and safety tips:

General Safety

1. Be aware of your surroundings: Stay alert and mindful of your belongings, especially in crowded areas.

2. Secure your valuables: Keep your wallet, purse, and phone secure. Using a cross-body bag or money belt can add extra security.

3. Avoid walking alone at night: Stick to well-lit areas and avoid deserted streets, particularly in the early morning hours.

4. Trust your instincts: If something feels off, avoid the situation and seek help from a trusted source.

Sun and Heat

1. Stay hydrated: Drink plenty of water throughout the day, especially in hot and humid weather.

2. Wear sunscreen: Use sunscreen with an SPF of 30 or higher and reapply frequently, especially after swimming or sweating.

3. Seek shade: Plan activities to avoid the peak heat of the day, typically between 11:00 AM and 3:00 PM. Take breaks in air-conditioned spaces.

4. Wear appropriate clothing: Choose loose-fitting, breathable clothing made from natural fibres like cotton or linen. Light-coloured clothes help reflect the sun's rays.

5. Beware of mosquitoes: Use insect repellent to avoid mosquito bites, especially during summer and fall.

Food and Water Safety

1. Choose reputable restaurants: Opt for places with good hygiene standards and avoid street vendors with questionable food handling practices.
2. Be cautious with raw shellfish: If you have concerns about allergies or freshness, choose cooked seafood options.
3. Drink bottled water: While tap water is generally safe, some visitors prefer bottled water for peace of mind.

Personal Health

1. Pack medications: Bring necessary prescription medications and consider packing over-the-counter remedies for minor ailments.
2. Purchase travel insurance: This can provide peace of mind in case of medical emergencies or trip cancellations.
3. Be aware of allergies: Inform restaurant staff about any allergies and carry an EpiPen if needed.
4. Wash your hands frequently: Regular hand washing is essential to prevent the spread of germs, especially before eating and after using the restroom.

Emergency Services

1. Dial 911 in emergencies: This connects you to medical services, police, or fire departments.

2. Know your nearest hospital: Research the location of the nearest hospital to your accommodation in case of a medical emergency.

Conclusion

New Orleans has cast its enchanting spell. You've explored the vibrant streets, immersed yourself in the infectious rhythms, and savoured the city's unique flavours. From the majestic Mississippi River to the haunting jazz melodies in the French Quarter, New Orleans has revealed its captivating soul.

While this book has been your guide, the true adventure lies beyond its pages. As you leave, carry with you the memories, the friendships, and the spirit of the Big Easy that has undoubtedly touched your heart.

New Orleans lingers. The melody of a brass band may resurface in your mind, the aroma of beignets may spark a craving, or the sight of a wrought-iron balcony may transport you back to a charming street corner. This is the enduring magic of New Orleans, a city that stays with you long after you've left.

Final Thoughts to Ponder

1. What surprised you most about New Orleans?
2. What local experiences resonated with you the most?
3. What hidden gems did you discover on your own?

New Orleans thrives on exploration. Let this book be a springboard for future adventures. There's always something new to discover in the Big Easy, from hidden jazz clubs to fascinating historical sites. Keep the spirit of New Orleans alive, and remember, there's always lagniappe (a little something extra) around the corner.

Printed in Great Britain
by Amazon